SAFE-GUARDING the children

Urgent Needs • Practical Steps • Spiritual Solutions

SAFE-GUARDING the children

Urgent Needs • Practical Steps • Spiritual Solutions

reports from
The Christian Science Monitor

articles from
The Christian Science Journal
and
Christian Science Sentinel

The Christian Science Publishing Society
Boston, Massachusetts, U.S.A.

Publisher's Note:
The articles in this book reprinted from *The Christian Science Monitor* use pseudonyms for minors and offenders.

Publisher's Cataloging-in-Publication
(Provided by Quality Books, Inc.)

Safeguarding the children : urgent needs, practical steps, spiritual
   solutions. — 1st ed.
     p. cm.
     Includes bibliographical references.
     Preassigned LCCN: 97-75057
     ISBN: 0-87510-335-9

    1. Child welfare. 2. Christian Science.
HV713.S34 1997   362.7
                            QBI97-41312

Contents

Foreword

Children face dangers everywhere. Ask parents, teachers, and law enforcement personnel in any country. Ask any kid, anywhere.

Dangers are not just in big cities. In places once considered safe—suburbs, rural areas, schools, even behind locked doors at home—children often contend with serious threats to their well-being and security. Today's pressures on families leave too many children on their own too much, often amid a swirl of bad influences.

Magazines and books, broadcast, film, and computer-driven media push images and messages at children—and adults—that promote violence and sexual indulgence. In the United States, gun violence among young people has increased dramatically, while in other countries, violent incidents involving children are no less disturbing. To be able to say with confidence, "*My* kids are good kids," is not enough. Children who have stayed free of drugs and alcohol may still find themselves victims of peers or adults who have not.

But it's not all bleakness and despair. Agencies long dedicated to protecting children are adapting to these aggressive threats, and redoubling their efforts to implement solutions. New initiatives and strategies are emerging. There is progress.

To examine these problems and the work being done to solve them, The Christian Science Publishing Society launched a media series entitled "Safeguarding the Children." Issues, ideas, and solutions were explored comprehensively in print, radio, and online formats.

The Christian Science Monitor, the award-winning international newspaper, featured extensive coverage ranging from the battle to end child prostitution to the controversy over violent programming on TV and the Internet. Sometimes unsettling, the *Monitor* reports present an unflinching look at the extent of the problems, and the actions under way to reverse the trends. These issues were also addressed in several of the *Monitor's* daily Home Forum page religious articles.

The "Safeguarding the Children" series was also developed in two magazines: *The Christian Science Journal*, a monthly magazine dedicated to recording the practicality of Christian healing, and *Christian Science Sentinel*, a weekly magazine that watches trends from a spiritual perspective. This is the first time that a series in these periodicals has run concurrently with a *Monitor* series on the same topic. Looking at these threats and challenges from a spiritual perspective, the *Sentinel* and *Journal* writers offer powerful, practical truths to comfort, encourage, and heal. A number of writers explain how spiritual insights brought decisive healing to a variety of dangerous conditions faced by young people and families.

The "Safeguarding" series was published in 1996, but the ongoing work is as current as today's news. Included in the last chapter of this book is a subsequent *Monitor* article about the role of citizen volunteers in this vital activity, paired with a *Sentinel* article from the series. For those seeking up-to-the-minute information about some of these topics, an appendix lists Internet addresses of many organizations dedicated to children's issues.

The dangers confronting children point to an urgent need for decisive action, moral courage, and spiritual growth. In this book you'll find reports on troubling current events, and counterbalancing them, you'll find articles filled with solid spiritual insights and dependable, healing truths.

We hope this book will inform, inspire, and support those individuals all around the world who are working to safeguard the children.

J. Anthony Periton
Editor-in-Chief
The Christian Science Publishing Society

Chapter 1

Working
to Keep Children Safe

Working with Young People to Make Their Lives Safer

David
Holmstrom

Staff Writer
The Christian Science Monitor

BOSTON—It could be a child's most basic need today: to feel safe in a world where caution is the watchword. The threat of violence sits high on the list of concerns both for kids in the suburbs and those negotiating the tough streets of the inner city.

For Felipé De Santos, growing up in Philadelphia's troubled inner city, safety did not exist in word or concept. His reality was gangs and dangerous streets.

"When all you know is danger, then you don't know about safety. You hang out with squads, smoking weed, using drugs," he says of street life. "You think it's normal, because that's all you know. Then you leave Philly, and come back, and wow! You say, 'Get me outta here!'"

Mr. De Santos is out of Philly now, living in Massachusetts, with a wife and baby. "It's boring," he says with a laugh, "but it's safe, and I'm starting my life over." Although he spent some time in juvenile detention, De Santos did not become just another numbing violence statistic—the kind that are causing concern across the country:

- Children 19 and under are killed with guns at the rate of 15 a day in the United States, according to the National Center for Health Statistics.
- The number of juveniles murdered in 1994 was 47 percent greater than in 1980, while overall murders rose only 1 percent during that period, according to the Campaign for an Effective Crime Policy.
- The majority of juvenile violent crimes are committed between 3 PM and 6 PM. Three out of 10 homicides by juveniles are killings of other children.
- Children ages 12 to 17 are 5 times more likely to be murder victims than adults older than 35.

Behind these statistics lie complex social and economic issues that have persisted for years. Experts disagree over the causes of youth violence and whether or not solutions will come from harsher penalties or increased attempts at early education and prevention.

2

Some believe the key contributing factor is the inability of some families to provide their children with steady love and clear values. In addition, critics charge the media with distorting the prevalence of violence through sensationalized reporting. And violent TV and movies are blamed for influencing teen behavior.

But despite differences over the causes, parents, educators, community groups, and legislators are devoting increasing attention to stemming violence and fear in children's lives.

In this series, the *Monitor* examines effective, grass-roots actions young people and adults can take. Signs of progress abound: children are learning to deal with provocation without getting into fights; schools are getting rid of guns; churches and communities are working to stem drug use and help young people spend their after-school hours more productively; and families are working together to provide a safe environment in their neighborhoods.

Moving beyond legislative efforts, adults are recognizing the need for community and individual initiative—and are taking action to keep children out of harm's way.

Beyond the controversy over the sources of violence are the individual, daily experiences of youths. The great majority of children and young people today, regardless of their home address, have not been shot, abused, or joined gangs. Of all crimes in the United States over the last few years, only 13 percent were committed by teens. And of the 1,268 murders of children under 18 in 1994, about 70 percent were committed by adults, according to the FBI Uniform Crime Report.

But the prevalence of violence in or near young lives, or their fear of violence, is now the common denominator, despite new figures showing that violent crime has dropped for the second year in a row. Violent incidents simply occur today in a greater number of public locations—including schools, long considered a place of refuge and safety.

In the book *Children in Danger* (Jossey-Bass Publishers, San Francisco), lead author James Garbarino writes about one boy desperately wanting to be safe. Living in Boston's inner city, the boy kept an empty deodorant bottle by his bed because the bottle said "guaranteed 100 percent safe."

But other young people respond by inuring themselves to violence, trying to shut it out while remaining dubious about their ability to eradicate its presence. "You can't help but be desensitized by violence," says Mary Harris, a teenager from Brockton, Massachusetts, who has a summer job in Boston with the Boston Initiative for Teen Pregnancy Prevention. "If you weren't desensitized, you would be jumping every second," she says. "I don't even try to feel safe, because once you do, something happens. But I'm watchful because you can't be dumb. Being safe means not having to be on duty."

For Maria Baptista-Jones, a teen living on her own in Boston's Jamaica Plain area, and also working for the Boston Initiative, violence has never been far away. "A couple of my friends have died from shootings," she says. "It's normal. This is a big city, and this is how people react. I feel like it is so common that now you take it as it comes to you, and you just keep moving on, one step at a time."

Outside the inner city, the threat of violence is often less immediate. In Brighton, 11-year-old Thomas Chan says violence isn't a problem in his school. "But kids learn fast," he says, "and sometimes they can't stop if they get involved in violence. It's like trying to cheat on a test. The first time someone tries it, it's hard. The second time is easier."

It is at such junctions that concerned adults can exercise a powerful and positive influence in educating young children about right and wrong—a factor increasingly reflected in the calls for more grass-roots involvement and caring on the part of adults.

Three adults made a difference for Polly Peterson, a self-described troublemaker in elementary school in Boston. "I was always fighting, and my principal and a program director finally opened me up, made me ask myself, 'What am I doing?' And my mom is my role model now because she went through so much."

But moral suasion has been accompanied by more somber efforts to discourage disruptiveness and violence. Many schools have become fortresses, with metal detectors, security guards, and drug-sniffing dogs. Strict rules for everything from clothing to gum are used.

But too often, in the well-intentioned attempt to create safety, the efforts are top-down, with no student involvement in decisions. The result is often a message that teachers and administrators are afraid of students. "A lot of the schools, teachers, and administrators we deal with," says Lori Frantz-Kannally, program director of Youth to Youth in Columbus, Ohio, "are finding out that to be successful in any of their school activities, they need to set up something like substance-free policies to help make the environment safe for kids, but also to let youths take leadership roles, to empower them to lead things. You have to listen to them."

Betty Ann Good agrees. After 10 years as president of Youth Crime Watch of America in Miami, she has concluded that security guards and metal detectors don't necessarily make a school safe.

Instead, the more that youths are encouraged to invest their ideas in programs, the more a school benefits.

"It is the atmosphere of the school," she says, "and whether or not the students' fears and concerns are being addressed. The young people are the most vulnerable, and they feel they don't have the power to change things."

Youth Crime Watch has helped create youth-led programs in 16 states that help free schools of crime and drugs.

"First, students identify what the problems are, and then they work to solve the problems," says Ms. Good. "They organize with student patrols and report crime because it is the right thing to do."

Students on the patrol have been trained in conflict resolution and mentoring. "A safe school is one where the students have a great deal of school spirit because they know they have made a difference," Good says. "More than anyone else, they want to make the changes."

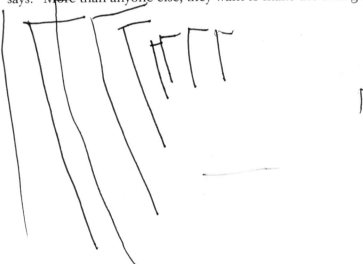

Culprits Are Alcohol, Drugs, Parental Actions, Teens Say

Marilyn Gardner

Staff Writer
The Christian Science Monitor

BOSTON—For a growing number of teenagers, concentrating on the 3 Rs may be taking second place to worrying about the 2 Gs—guns and gangs.

Ten percent of teens surveyed in a new national poll say they are afraid of being shot or hurt by other teens carrying guns in school. And more than 40 percent say they know other teenagers who are members of gangs.

The survey, commissioned by Children's Institute International, a nonprofit organization in Los Angeles, polled 904 teenagers between the ages of 12 and 17. Nearly half of these students think their school is getting more violent, and a quarter think their neighborhood is less safe. These perceptions hold true among both girls and boys in all kinds of school settings—inner cities, suburbs, rural areas—and in all regions of the country.

"One of the things we don't know from this kind of survey is the actual level of violence," says Mary Emmons, president of Children's Institute International. "But perception in many ways is reality, because we make decisions based on our perceptions. We gear our lives based on that. We're seeing that kids are reacting to what they perceive to be a more violent world."

Like adults, Ms. Emmons says, children "are adjusting their lives because of their fear of violence. We heard children telling us they will take a longer route to school. They will not involve themselves in certain school activities. They are afraid that if they go to a certain activity or take a certain route to school, they'll end up getting mugged or worse."

Yet blame for violence cannot always be placed on strangers or peers. In one of the most significant findings, 43 percent of the teens say that they think violence is learned from parents. In addition, 85 percent believe that drugs and alcohol are important causes of violence within families as well as among young people.

6

Fourteen percent of teenagers recommend banning or controlling violence in entertainment. And 12 percent suggest banning or controlling weapons by using metal detectors and other devices. But 16 percent say there is no hope.

Emmons refutes that notion. "There are many good things that can be done," she says. She cites a zero-tolerance policy in Michigan, in which students who take a weapon to school are expelled for the first offense. "If kids know there is sure and swift action, they are willing to turn kids in. But if they're not sure the kids are going to be kicked out of school, they're unwilling to tell, because they're putting themselves in danger."

Parents, educators, and police all need to be "a lot more involved," Emmons adds. "Kids tell us it makes a big difference if parents are involved in their schools. They also want schools to have strict rules and old-fashioned methods of discipline, to make sure principals and teachers are really in control of their schools."

Teens Speak Out

Feature
The Christian Science Monitor

Choosing a Better Way

"I Know I Don't Need to Fight"

Maria Baptista-Jones lives on her own in Boston's Jamaica Plain neighborhood. A peer counselor at Boston Initiative for Teen Pregnancy Prevention, she holds two jobs.

"Some of my family members tried to lean me toward violence and pushed me to be a fighter," says the 17-year-old, who is tall, full of humor and good-natured aggression. "'You're big; use your size,' they would say. 'If anybody gets in your way, just hit 'em, hit 'em, hit 'em.' But I understand that this came from their parents teaching them violence. I also had family members who said, 'No, Maria, violence is inappropriate. You have to do it another way.' They helped me to understand how I would feel if I were in the other person's shoes. . . . I know I could fight and really hurt someone, but I know now that I don't need to. . . .

"One of my teachers named Agnes helped me, too. She was like a big sister and said her home was always open to me. She said just because I'm big and have always been a tomboy, that it didn't mean I had to be rough and aggressive. I could key myself down and get the right perspective and really help other people in my community.

"I dress real funky, and I'll change my style every day, and if a girl says, 'Oh that's a cute outfit,' there you go. You can be my friend from that one comment. I'm the type of person who goes on the train and talks to everybody. Ten years from now, I want to have three kids, a big house, and be in politics. There is so much I want to do in my life I don't know if I can fit it in one life span . . . I was a child of DSS (the Massachusetts Department of Social Services). I grew up in the system, and I want to change everything about it."

Laying a Solid Foundation

"A Teacher Inspired Me"

Mary Harris lives in Brockton, Massachusetts, with her parents. She travels to a private school in Braintree, and goes to church every Sunday.

"I had a teacher in elementary school who inspired me," says the 16-year-old. "She didn't focus on violence, but she laid the foundation for everything you should learn, from morals, to self-esteem, to loving yourself. Every morning we would recite this saying that would reinforce self-esteem, and a lot of times that kept me going: 'Is this going to work for my benefit or my downfall?'

"I got a lot from my parents in morals, in church, and that keeps me out of a lot of things in my surroundings. I'm the type of a person who wouldn't get in a fight. No need for me; it wouldn't help me with anything. In 10 years, I want to have a master's degree and be working toward my doctorate in psychology with a special emphasis in child development. I want to know why and how kids do things, but right now I don't want any kids of my own. I'll be married and living in Virginia— but no kids, unless my husband has something to say."

"Violence Is a Learned Behavior"

Polly Peterson lives with her mother in the Dorchester section of Boston. She goes to school in East Boston. Polly is also a peer counselor at the Boston Initiative for Teen Pregnancy Prevention.

"Yeah, I feel safe, but I know anything could happen to me," the 15-year-old says. "I never had a problem in my community with violence, or violence coming up to me, unless I caused it or started something.

"Violence is a learned behavior, and everybody learns some kind of violence. You can't stop it completely; you can only reduce it.

"The media have a problem with judging certain communities and minorities who live there. If a whole lot of Puerto Ricans live there, nothing but babies; if blacks, then nothing but gangs. The media is really wrong with stereotypes like that.

"In school we should have more mediation, more teachers and mentors acting one-on-one with kids. When I was a kid, and angry and didn't want to talk, this lady sat with me in school, and she figured out what was wrong by using dolls. I would show her what was happening on the dolls, and I would punch the dolls. I don't know what I want to be 10 years from now. I don't have a clue, but I want to be able to influence people for good, and work with computers."

Around the world, images of child exploitation are pervasive. Anything that prompts action against it is helpful, but sometimes the magnitude of the problem is daunting.

We can help the children of the world with prayer, and it's important to start by recognizing children's true status. If we hold children to be just small, undeveloped, biochemical beings, we may be trapped into thinking of them as always risking attack and deception. But if we are able to see them differently—spiritually, as God created them—we can recognize that they have inherent strength and invulnerability.

God created each individual in His image and likeness. This identity is not material and mortal. It is spiritual and perfect, like God Himself. God's creation is finished. Nothing that He created has to become His image—whatever He creates is immediately and eternally complete.

Every individual God created reflects each quality of His, even as each work of a certain artist reflects the artist's particular style. God's "style," the Godliness reflected in everything He creates, includes peace, strength, intelligence, love, invulnerability. It is only good, because God is only good. God couldn't create anything or anyone without those attributes. It's just not His style. He wouldn't create one work of art capable of hurting or attacking another. Each of us already has all that is good; good does not come to us as a result of our getting older or physically bigger.

Christ Jesus taught this. Once, when some children were brought to him to be blessed, Jesus' disciples attempted to turn them away (see Mark 10:13–16). In that time adulthood was respected, while youth was often disregarded. But Jesus taught his disciples something new. He explained that in order to receive the kingdom of God, one must become "as a little child." The Bible says, "And he took [the children] up in his arms, put his hands upon them, and blessed them."

Children Are Not Victims

Religious Article
The Home Forum
The Christian Science Monitor

The book *Science and Health with Key to the Scriptures* explains the spiritual message of the Bible, including the teachings of Jesus. Mary Baker Eddy, the Discoverer of Christian Science, wrote in it, "Jesus loved little children because of their freedom from wrong and their receptiveness of right" (p. 236). This "freedom from wrong" comes from strength, not vulnerability. As we recognize all children as always connected to the one Father-Mother God, we can expect to see evidence that He is speaking directly to them, guiding them away from danger and into safety. Each child has a direct link to wisdom. Not one has to "grow up" to get it. It is inherent always.

When my daughter was small, her father and I separated. After having been in a two-parent household with a stay-at-home mother, she had to face moving, being apart from her father, full-time day care, and having a working mother. I had heard that abrupt changes of this sort in a child's life are often thought to cause emotional damage.

But in preparing for her birth some years before, my husband and I had studied Christian Science, to learn about her true origin as God's perfect child. She was not our creation then, nor was she now the cumulative result of our human influence on her—she was complete, with her own identity, established by God. That foundational prayer, recalled, enabled me to understand her as completely unharmed by the changes that came from our new circumstances.

As the years have progressed, I have been so grateful that our daughter has never displayed the behavioral or emotional problems sometimes associated with broken homes. In fact, when I have mentioned the situation to her schoolteachers, they have invariably responded with surprise. She is a delightful, normal child, full of joy and love of life.

The completeness of each of our children is established and intact. Its source is in God. When our prayers for children foster this conviction, we bring out increasing evidence of every individual's freedom from wrong. Let's join together to bring more of this understanding to our world.

Their faces speak to us, the faces of the world's children portrayed in news reports and on magazine covers. Often they are the faces of children involved in tragedies that no one should ever have to experience. What can we do when we long to heal these children's hurts, to save them from abusive situations, and to rescue them from the wars and famines of the world's making?

We can more deeply cherish the qualities of purity and innocence, which are inherent in children, and, actually, in all of us—qualities from God. These are qualities that the world does not seem to value. Providing a supportive environment for the development and protection of these qualities in children is not generally a priority in society. The simple, pure child thought, instead of being valued as a strength, is more often associated with vulnerability.

But the qualities that make up childlike thought—innocence, purity, trust, and spontaneity—are not weak and vulnerable. They are the very expression of God revealing Himself to mankind. They carry with them the power and reality of their divine source. Hatred, evil, anger, crudity, sensualism, have no source in God or Truth and thus no power to overrule the nature of God expressed in man.

So we can support children by refusing to equate their true nature with vulnerability and helplessness.

We also can challenge the world's view of where control and governance lie. Each individual, no matter what his or her age or position, is truly under the only power there is—the all-loving, infinite Mind, God. This truth can be demonstrated in even the most challenging human situation, as was illustrated in the Bible when the Egyptian Pharaoh decreed that all male babies should be murdered. Think of the inspired listening to God's direction by Moses' mother, which led her to place the baby Moses in an ark of bulrushes by the river's edge. There, he was found and raised by the Pharaoh's daughter—thus

Cherishing the World's Children

Harriet Barry Schupp

Contributor
Christian Science Sentinel

ensuring not only his safety but the fulfillment of his great spiritual purpose (see Ex. 2:1–10). Each child today has a grand spiritual purpose, and our mothering thought, recognizing God's control over each of His ideas, can help foil the attempts of evil to thwart that purpose.

Whether we are parents or not, we have a responsibility to express the parenting nature of our Father-Mother God. This parenting begins in our own thought as we watch over just what concepts we allow to have a place there regarding children. Is it helpful to the world's children if we are believing that anyone is separate from God and operating independently? Is it helpful if we believe that life is in matter and at the disposal of material circumstances?

God's children are not defenseless little people subject to the mistakes and cruelty of big people. They are complete spiritual ideas, not needing to mature materially in order to have the protection and strength of divine Mind.

In *Science and Health*, there is a description of children, which reads in part, "The spiritual thoughts and representatives of Life, Truth, and Love" (p. 582). What power and invulnerability come with this true identity of children! Because they represent Life, they cannot be deprived of life, vitality, joy. As representatives of Truth, they cannot be demoralized by injustice, dishonesty, or erroneous concepts about them. As Love's pure representatives, they are not polluted by sensualism, nor can they be deprived of tenderness and protection. Affirming these truths invokes the power of the Christ presence in the midst of whatever situation children are in.

Jesus made a point of recognizing the godliness of childlikeness. He said, "Suffer the little children to come unto me, and forbid them not: for such is the kingdom of God." And then, remarkably, he showed just how important were qualities such as receptivity and humility by saying, "Verily I say unto you, Whosoever shall not receive the kingdom of God as a little child, he shall not enter therein" (Mark 10:14, 15).

We need to stand up for the presence of a childlikeness everywhere — and especially in our own thinking. We each are daily contributing to the world's atmosphere of thought. "Beloved children," Mary Baker Eddy once said in an address to her Church, "the world has need of you, — and more as children than as men and women: it needs your innocence, unselfishness, faithful affection, uncontaminated lives" (*Miscellaneous Writings*, p. 110).

The spiritual fact is that childlikeness is a quality of everyone. No one can really lose or destroy this innate Godlike nature. We are not little mortals or big mortals or anywhere in between. We are immortal children of God.

Chapter

Stopping

Family Violence

2

Efforts to End Abuse Open Doors for Troubled Families

Marilyn Gardner

Staff Writer
The Christian Science Monitor

BOSTON—Ellie Douglas always wanted her son and daughter to have what she didn't have as a child—a father. Even though her husband beat her regularly, she endured the abuse to keep her family together.

But that tenuous arrangement ended five years ago when Ms. Douglas's husband threatened to kill her by putting a garbage bag over her head and tying a rope around her neck. She and her children, then ages 7 and 2, fled with only the clothes on their backs, seeking refuge in a shelter for battered women.

"Because of the children—that's why I stayed with my husband as long as I did," explains Douglas, of Clearwater, Florida, noting that he never harmed the children. "As it turned out, that wasn't the best thing for me to do."

Determining "the best thing to do" to protect children from family violence raises anguished questions not only for mothers, but also for concerned professionals. Even when children are not physically abused, they often become frightened observers of the violence inflicted on a battered parent, nearly always their mother.

"Children witness a great deal of parental violence," says David Finkelhor, codirector of the Family Research Laboratory at the University of New Hampshire in Durham. Research suggests, he adds, that children exposed to domestic violence are more likely to be aggressive with schoolmates and grow up to be abusers or victims in their own relationships. Surveys also show that teenagers themselves say that young people learn violent behavior most often from what they see at home.

The Family Research Laboratory estimates that violent episodes occur in 1 out of 8 marriages in a given year. Experts say that 95 percent of that violence is perpetrated by men.

Children surrounded by domestic violence can be hurt in three ways, according to Janet Carter, managing associate director of the Family Violence

Prevention Fund in San Francisco. "They can be physically injured if they get caught in the fray between the parents," she says. "They can be intentionally injured by the perpetrator in his attempt to control the adult victim. He'll say, 'If I can't get to you, I'll get to what you love most.' Finally, even if they're not physically injured, there's a lot of emotional effect."

Douglas knows that firsthand. After she left her husband, her son became very angry. His grades plummeted from A's and B's to D's and F's, and she had to seek counseling for him.

Until recently, counselors and social workers have treated child abuse and domestic violence as separate problems, handled by completely different systems — one set up to protect children, the other to protect women. "Child abuse and neglect, when they are reported, are investigated by an official state agency," explains Susan Schechter, a professor at the University of Iowa School of Social Work in Iowa City. "Domestic violence has traditionally been dealt with in small, grassroots services. Yet in 30 to 50 percent of child abuse cases, there's also domestic violence."

(While government studies indicate child abuse and neglect cases doubled between 1986 and 1993 [to 2.8 million], researchers say much of the increase likely results from increased reporting.)

Calling the two forms of family violence "inextricably linked," Ms. Carter says, "Until we address both problems together, we're not really addressing the safety of the family." Adds Susan Kelly, director of family preservation services at the Michigan Family Independence Agency in Lansing, "Child-welfare and domestic-violence agencies have the same goals. The first goal is safety, then justice for children and justice for victims, and finally peace — safe homes, safe relationships."

As first steps in collaboration, the Massachusetts Department of Social Services hired 11 domestic-violence specialists to work alongside child protection workers. Michigan also has a statewide collaborative effort, called Families First.

Two years ago, the National Council of Juvenile and Family Court Judges in Reno, Nevada, published a "Model State Code on Domestic and Family Violence" to encourage consistency in family-violence legislation. Since then, says Merry Hofford, director of the project, a number of states have done a side-by-side comparison of their statutes with the model code and have made adjustments.

"The way to make a child safe is to make the mom safe, by protecting women through laws, shelters, safe housing, and legal advocacy," says Linda Osmundson, executive director of the Center Against Spouse Abuse in St. Petersburg, Florida. "Very often a mom is accused of failing to protect a child, when she can't even protect herself."

Despite these encouraging signs, some family violence programs face financial challenges that could limit their work. "It's getting really tough these days," says Ms. Osmundson. "Federal and state funding has been pushed down to the local level. That puts us in competition with other programs."

Still, as public awareness of the problem grows, various efforts seek to help victims of abuse, men who batter, and children affected by parental violence. The National Domestic Abuse Hotline (800-799-SAFE) based in Austin, Texas, has provided help and referrals for more than 60,000 callers since opening in February, says supervisor Liz Leslie. The nonprofit Domestic Abuse Project in Minneapolis, which helps youngsters who have witnessed domestic violence, is being replicated elsewhere in the United States and in other countries.

Other efforts focus on prevention. A home visitation program sponsored by the Kempe Center in Denver visits 3,000 families a year, offering support after the birth of a baby and before violence can occur. "European countries provide this service routinely," says Susan Hiatt, director. "In this country, we require more training and education to drive a car than we do to have a family." Some schools, both public and private, now include discussions of family and dating violence in health and family life classes.

Religious groups are also active. The World Council of Churches has its new Program to Overcome Violence, aimed at identifying effective church programs. Women in the United Methodist Church are focusing on domestic violence issues. And Jewish Women International in Washington has distributed 3,000 copies of a resource guide for rabbis on domestic violence. A conference at Brandeis University in Waltham, Massachusetts, addressed the topic, "The Inside Story of Abuse in the Jewish Home."

"So many efforts are directed to intervention after the fact," says Rabbi Julie Spitzer, director of the UAHC Greater New York Council of Reform Synagogues in New York. "The work we do in prevention is so much more valuable. If we can teach children, for example, that it's not right for the person who says they love you to hit you, or for you to hit the person you love, that has benefits in geometric proportion to saying, after the fact, 'What you did was wrong.'"

As such efforts expand, family-violence professionals hope societal attitudes will change, making tolerance of family violence unacceptable. Meanwhile, women like Douglas show the possibilities for building violence-free lives for themselves and their children. Today Douglas, an executive secretary, describes her life as "great" and her home as "very peaceful." "My son understands he's going to grow up respecting women," Douglas says. "And my daughter is going to grow up realizing she is not supposed to take abuse from anybody."

Osmundson sums up her hope for change. "We can begin to help people operate in an egalitarian family setting, where there is shared decision making, and where children are disciplined with means other than violence," she says. "If we can teach children that violence is not an option, if we can teach families that there are nonviolent ways to solve problems, we can become models for our neighborhood and our community. We have to start with our families, finding peace at home before we have peace in the world. That's the big vision."

Connecting the Dots: Men Find Antidote for Anger

Marilyn Gardner

Staff Writer
The Christian Science Monitor

BOSTON—It happened in an instant one Sunday afternoon. A six-year-old girl and her four-year-old brother were playing in their Minneapolis home when suddenly, the little boy punched his sister. The provocation angered their father, and without thinking, he slapped his son as punishment.

The next day, the boy's teacher noticed red marks on his face. Following Minnesota law, she reported it to the Department of Child Protection Services. Although the agency closed the case after a police investigation, it recommended that the father, Tom Mason, enroll in an anger-management program for help in dealing constructively with his anger.

"I took their advice, because I'm not the type who hits my kids," says Mr. Mason. "I figured, if I did that, there's something that needs to be looked at. When it happened, I stood back and said, 'What did I do?' It actually scared me. It was an overreaction."

Although Mason's slap was a one-time mistake, that kind of overreaction fuels countless explosive incidents that injure and endanger women and children. By helping men learn to control their anger, the Fathers' Resource Center in Minneapolis, which sponsors the class, hopes to prevent violence in the home or stop it if it already exists. The 2½-hour classes meet weekly.

Getting more men enrolled in classes like this, as well as in batterer-intervention programs designed to help men stop being abusive, remains a goal of many counselors. About half the participants attend the 16-week program because of a court order. Others are referred by wives or girlfriends.

"They usually haven't connected the dots," says program leader Mark Toogood. "They know what they experienced themselves as kids, but for many, it is a light bulb [going on] to see that they are replicating the same behaviors they swore they would never do, that they themselves endured as children."

One class participant, Phil Austin, says his first marriage failed because of his anger. Many in the group, he finds, "just feel good that they have a place to go to talk, because so much of what men learn is about not expressing their feelings. Men have never explored other ways to express their anger other than violently or in the context of power and control."

Lawrence Roberts enrolled to deal with anger in his second marriage. "The whole idea is to take responsibility for yourself. . . . There's no way you can be angry at your spouse and not affect your children. When you're angry with someone in the family and you don't deal with it effectively, it doesn't go away."

Although other social service groups in Minnesota are copying the male anger program, many lament the overall lack of services for men. "This class is something I wish I had had when I was a lot younger," Roberts says. "Someone who could have said to me, 'This is how life is, and this is how you handle certain situations.' I do believe if there were more men's anger groups, there would be a lot less abuse."

Crisis Nurseries Help Parents in Tough Times

Andrea Neighbours

Special to
The Christian Science Monitor

BOSTON—Ted White seemed set up for failure. A single parent in recovery from alcohol and drug abuse, Mr. White had just gotten his three children back from state custody in Oregon. He had no car and few resources to support his family.

To make matters worse, his needs weren't being met in his 12-step program. "I'd go with the kids, and there'd be smoking, swearing and behaviors I didn't want the kids to see," Mr. White recalls.

Then a friend led him to Relief Nursery in Eugene, Oregon—one of a growing number of programs across the nation designed to stop child abuse and neglect before they occur and help families stay together. Through Relief Nursery, White started receiving home visits for help with parenting and recovery. To enable White to attend the nursery's peer support group, Parents in Recovery, the nursery sent a van to pick up White and his kids and provided a light meal and child care during the group session.

"I don't know where I'd be right now without the support of the nursery," he says. "It provided a safe place to come, with transportation."

Prevention is increasingly billed as a common-sense and cost-effective antidote to American society's problems. Communities in almost every state have started crisis nurseries.

The idea is simple: Give parents a break from kids. In addition to taking children for 36 hours or longer while parents work through a crisis, most nurseries also offer comprehensive services for the whole family, including early childhood programs at the nursery and at home, parent training, support for families going through divorce or other crises, and programs for families dealing with substance abuse.

"When a . . . parent is close to . . . doing something harmful, it's common sense that they need to take a break" from their kids, says Stanley Turecki, author of "The Emotional Problems of Normal Children." Since 1988, when funds became available for the

Temporary Child Care for Children with Disabilities and Crisis Nurseries Act (TCCA), the federal government has given out nearly 100 grants totaling more than $30 million to get crisis nurseries up and running. But even with these new programs, many crisis nurseries are unable to keep up with demand and have to place families on waiting lists, according to a 1991 study.

Relief Nursery, started in 1976, has grown from serving children in 8 to 10 families to helping nearly 100 children and their families each year. Its waiting list includes several hundred names.

"Crisis care is an integral component of saving [some families] from destruction—and a whole lot cheaper than placing that child in foster care for a year," says Sue McKinney-Cull at the ARCH National Resource Center for Respite and Crises Care Services, in Chapel Hill, North Carolina.

"Communities are crying out for prevention alternatives that reach families before a child winds up dead in the emergency room or removed from the home for sexual abuse," says Jeanne Landdeck-Sisco, director of Casa de los Niños—the country's first crisis nursery—located in Phoenix.

In its 23rd year, Casa de los Niños has 58 beds for children, from newborns to 12-year-olds. Parents are often at the poverty level or lower. Many are single mothers. All face at least one crisis that makes good parenting difficult. "They may be homeless, involved in domestic violence, about to enter drug treatment, or separated from their husband and completely without resources; or Mom may need to go into the hospital for an operation," says Ms. Landdeck-Sisco.

According to Relief Nursery, 99 percent of enrolled families are at the poverty level or have an extremely low income; 65 percent have a member with substance-abuse problems; 40 percent are single-parent households; and 24 percent have experienced homelessness in the last year.

One of the crisis nursery's most important functions may be understanding the context of some parents' actions. One day, for example, a woman ended up at Relief Nursery for tying her young children to a tree. It turned out she was afraid for their safety. "She was homeless and camping by a river. She was terrified those kids would run into the river and drown," says Executive Director Jean Phelps. "Before we put out the blame, we need to figure out what's going on. . . . We're really good listeners, and we have a broad array of programs to offer," she explains.

Most nurseries and parents hook up through referrals by public health and social service agencies, but there is also self-referral. "Parents call us up crying, saying, 'I need help. I don't want to hurt my child,'" Ms. Phelps says.

Crisis nurseries are proving themselves. A University of Iowa study showed a 13 percent decrease in the incidence of child abuse in seven counties with crisis nurseries. Relief Nursery reports that 90 percent of enrolled children were living safely with their families by the end of the year, and of the 11 percent in foster care, more than a quarter were able to return home.

"This is no finger-in-the dike solution," says Phelps. "We've been at this since 1976, and we know you truly can turn lives around with the participation of the families. People have to want to change, but then you have to create the programs that allow them to participate and make that change happen."

In search of an explanation of present difficulties, some people try delving into their past by means of a psychological technique called regression therapy. The assumption is that this is necessary to the successful establishment of a healthy, balanced outlook on life. The claim is also made that certain shortcomings or failures in an individual can be directly attributed to an abusive past. It's assumed that one who has been abused, physically or mentally, may find it difficult to cope with recurring, sometimes jarring memories.

A friend of the writer, at the age of three years, bore the brunt of severe parental domestic violence. Then he was abandoned on a street corner, along with his sister, who was one and a half years old. Their mother had put them out, and they never saw her again. They were placed in various other homes, sometimes with strangers who were even more abusive. Later in life, this friend reexamined many times what had happened in those earlier years in an attempt to sort out his concept of the world, searching for meaningful answers, but he faced what seemed a stone wall. It was a wall of frustration based on his belief that his history as a battered child had been allowed by a punishing God. The acceptance of this belief about God and His relation to him thwarted all his efforts to come out of the mire.

When, however, he was given a copy of *Science and Health with Key to the Scriptures* by Mary Baker Eddy and began to read it, the Scriptures became illuminated for him. Through consecrated study of this book in conjunction with the Bible and through daily prayer, he experienced permanent freedom from the belief that past injustices had power over him. The initial breakthrough came when he read with fresh insight Paul's statement, "Therefore if any man be in Christ, he is a new creature: old things are passed away; behold, all things are become new" (II Cor. 5:17). He realized he must see this more

Freedom from Past Abuse: Through Regression? Or Progression?

Frederick Sparrevohn May

Contributor
The Christian Science Journal

clearly and stop returning to the past, endeavoring to blame present failings on someone else.

Nowhere in the Bible does Christ Jesus ever recommend or practice the analysis of someone's past experience in order to restore that individual to wholeness. This, however, does not mean his disciples were not tempted to explore a false theory of cause and effect that was accepted in their times. Once they asked Jesus, "Master, who did sin, this man, or his parents, that he was born blind?" Jesus replied, "Neither hath this man sinned, nor his parents: but that the works of God should be made manifest in him" (John 9:2, 3). And Jesus went on to heal the man.

Whatever ghastly experience one seems to have gone through, placing blame on others is of no use in solving the problem of being. Instead, by looking straight ahead in our desire to know God and our relation to Him, and not stopping to analyze the supposed material causes of our own faults or those of others, we find harmony and freedom. *Science and Health* states: "Citizens of the world, accept the 'glorious liberty of the children of God,' and be free! This is your divine right" (*Science and Health*, p. 227). To claim this divine right requires self-examination, not self-criticism. All wrong belongs to the dream that life and intelligence begin and end in matter. As we awake from this dream and realize that sin, in whatever form or disguise, has never touched the child of God, we not only forgive but totally forget injustices perpetrated against us. This correct sense of man's nature opens wide the vision and enables one to cut through the illusion of a poor, sick, and sinning mortal, struggling with a history of pain. Our Father-Mother God supplies all good to His beloved reflection, man. Where, then, is the necessity of returning to a material past to eliminate something that was only a false belief in life separate from God?

As my friend found, it is useless to analyze the memory of past injustices, since they have no place in the divine Mind or in man, Mind's perfect reflection. Furthermore, healing in Christian Science is not a human effort to wipe out or adjust to a material past; rather, it is an awakening to the allness of good alone, as proclaimed by God. "And God saw every thing that he had made, and, behold, it was very good" (Gen. 1:31).

The recognition of good as the only power eliminates the belief that there is an opposing brute force or that God could allow evil to exist or operate. Understanding that there is but one power, God, good, the

All-in-all, and that man reflects this power, we become followers of good, which shields us from wrong. This divine power is implied in this question from the Bible: "And who is he that will harm you, if ye be followers of that which is good?" (I Pet. 3:13).

The child of God can never lose his identity or suffer loss or impairment of any kind. The safety of each of God's children is the result of the equipollence of God, which signifies equality of power at all points. Only God, good, is present at all times, in every place. Mrs. Eddy writes of the implications of what she discovered of God's nature: "The equipollence of God brought to light another glorious proposition, — man's perfectibility and the establishment of the kingdom of heaven on earth" (*Science and Health*, p. 110). Our real being has never been maligned in any way, is absolutely untouched, unmaimed, unstained, and unblamed. *Science and Health* states, "The temporal and unreal never touch the eternal and real" (*ibid.*, p. 300).

One definition of progression includes these words: "a moving forward or onward; progress"; while regression is defined as "a going back; return; movement backward." It's vitally important to choose rightly the direction in which we are heading. Progress toward total freedom from any belief that one has been wronged is assured us as we follow the behest of Paul: "Brethren, I count not myself to have apprehended: but this one thing I do, forgetting those things which are behind, and reaching forth unto those things which are before, I press toward the mark for the prize of the high calling of God in Christ Jesus" (Phil. 3:13, 14).

Chapter 3

Countering
the Danger of Guns

What Makes Children Choose to Use Guns?

David
Holmstrom

Staff Writer
The Christian Science Monitor

BOSTON—"Why is it that with all we have as a nation, some of our children are so eager to kill each other?" asks Joella Burgoon, executive director of the Gun Safety Institute in Cleveland.

One reason, according to a recent study by the institute of 1,164 third- through twelfth-graders, is that many children don't understand the distinction between being assertive in life and being aggressive toward people.

"The kids are telling us that what society is teaching them is that the most aggressive person is always the winner," says Ms. Burgoon, "and the ultimate aggression is the handgun."

The study was aimed at determining "what needs, goals, beliefs, and emotions are involved in the decision to carry a gun or behave aggressively." It identified four kinds of attitudes that make youths "prone" to gun use:

1. Guns and the people who use them are exciting;
2. Guns provide both safety and power;
3. Physical aggression is acceptable or comfortable behavior; and
4. If offended or shamed, one's pride can only be recovered by violent aggression.

The study also found a dramatic and somewhat puzzling increase in violence-prone attitudes between the fifth and sixth grades.

Among the children in the study, 50 percent had a family member who had been shot, and 5 percent had been shot themselves. Some 87 percent knew someone who had a gun.

After designing a two-week curriculum to respond directly to those "gun-proneness" factors and trying it in Cleveland schools, the institute found through an evaluation that little change in attitudes took place, even though teachers praised the program.

"We discovered we were not speaking to the kids well enough where they were, and even after great discussions, our point wasn't being made," says Ms. Burgoon. "Also, the more aggressive kids tended to shut down the less aggressive kids."

The curriculum, "Solutions Without Guns," is being redesigned to last a full semester and so that each lesson plan will have a clearly defined objective "with a finish to the discussions" and more explicitness about the interpersonal skills being taught. The "Understanding Kids' Motivation" revised curriculum will be used in fifth and sixth grade classes in 16 Cleveland schools beginning in February 1997.

"It taught us how little we all know about the way kids think," Burgoon says, regarding the first two-week effort. "We treated [guns and violence] like all the other things you teach them." But that's not a sufficient approach, she adds, "because there is a society out there that is teaching them a whole bunch of other things . . . that are intimately intertwined with their sense of self and being somebody in their world."

As violence among youths has risen, many schools and organizations across the United States have launched similar programs and curricula in recent years to try to teach a different reality about handguns and to change attitudes toward gun use.

Handgun Control Inc., the nation's largest gun-control lobbying organization, based in Washington, D.C., created the first "anti-gun" school curriculum for all ages called STAR (Straight Talk About Risks). "The program is used to give kids an opportunity to practice skills that get them out of situations where guns might be present," says Holly Richardson, a spokeswoman for STAR. While it is not a conflict-resolution program, it teaches youths to express their feelings and differences without resorting to guns. Some 80 school districts around the country use the program. "We are having trouble keeping up with requests," Ms. Richardson says. In the first two years of the program in Miami, the school district reported a one-third drop in gun injuries and deaths.

Hands Without Guns, a national organization that links with existing community groups, brings youths together to promote nonviolent and productive efforts already under way in communities. It also creates "spin-off" efforts to help launch new projects.

In Boston, Chicago, and Washington, D.C., youth workshops create positive TV spots about youths, conduct toy-gun turn-ins (450 toy guns in Boston were exchanged for books and other toys) and learn-ins, and support a variety of community and arts programs. The program is being evaluated by Harvard School of Public Health and the

Medical College of Wisconsin to determine the impact on young people's attitudes.

In Seattle, Mothers Against Violence in America has for the past two years offered SAVE (Students Against Violence Everywhere), a program in which students set up violence awareness chapters in their schools. Each school focuses on an aspect of violence, such as handguns, dating violence, or gang violence, and creates a program of prevention efforts. The program has grown rapidly, but has not yet had an overall evaluation.

BOSTON—He doesn't talk easily about it. But not too long after the third killing—this time in his family's apartment one afternoon in 1990—Michael McDonald finally cut through the weight of the violence he had lived through and was "pushed into action."

Two of his older brothers had been murdered several years earlier—one in a robbery attempt, the other inside prison walls. Another brother committed suicide. His mother had been wounded by a stray bullet in the neighborhood, and his sister was pushed off a roof and permanently injured. And now this, a shooting in his family's apartment in South Boston's Old Colony project where many large, Irish-American families live in poverty and under a code of silence.

Police accused Michael's little brother, Steven, of pulling the trigger of a .357 Magnum that struck down 13-year-old Tommy Vance. The two boys had been best friends, playing recklessly with a loaded gun. Steven was convicted of murder. Later a state court overturned the conviction because of discrepancies in the evidence.

But in the immediate aftermath, Michael McDonald changed from numb to clear. "I stepped back and looked at what violence did to my family of 11 kids," he says, softly. "As a survivor, I knew I had to do something to stop it."

Instead of succumbing to revenge or despair, he decided to work at bringing people together, to help communities break free of violence and handguns. And to help other survivors of violence.

The result, some six years later, is that McDonald, now program director of Citizens for Safety, a grassroots community organization, is one of Boston's most effective community workers. "I would do this work if I was paid or not," he says.

His most outstanding public effort so far is a gun buy-back program that has removed 2,600 handguns from Boston's streets in the last three years.

One Family's Trials Spur a Commitment to Community Safety

David Holmstrom

Staff Writer
The Christian Science Monitor

35

In addition, Citizens for Safety and McDonald are involved in three neighborhood projects: a basketball Peace League that also has job readiness and conflict resolution built into it, a peace curriculum in 10 schools using workshops to teach violence prevention, and a Hands Without Guns public service TV project organized by youths, which depicts teens at work in communities.

"Citizens for Safety has grown into a kind of Safety program coalition-convener that brings citywide resources to projects," says Harlan Jones, the group's executive director. All the organization's funds come from private foundations.

"Michael is probably the most committed individual I've ever met," says Bob Sege, a pediatrician at Tufts University School of Medicine in Medford, Massachusetts, and a board member of Citizens for Safety.

In March this year, McDonald was one of six Boston activists awarded $20,000 each from the Philanthropic Initiative, a nonprofit organization that sends anonymous "spotters" in the community to find unsung heroes.

"He's a rare collaborator," says Joan Sweeney, Director of Public Safety Consulting for the Boston Management Consortium. "He can hold his own with lots of different kinds of people without slamming other people's perspectives. There is no way that anyone working with him over time would ever question his commitment to solving the problems."

Firearms have become the weapon of choice
for growing numbers of young people.

200,000,000	firearms owned by Americans
25	children die every two days from gunshot wounds
208	children under 10 are killed each year in incidents involving firearms
In 1979, **1,644**	children aged 1 to 19 were killed in firearm homicides
In 1993, **3,647**	children aged 1 to 19 were killed in firearm homicides
13%	of murder victims in urban areas are under 18
21%	of high school students say they know someone who has died violently
28%	of youths who have carried weapons have witnessed violence in their homes
73%	of high school students consider teenage violence and crime to be a major problem

Sources: The FBI, the US Department of Justice, American Demographics Inc., Children's Defense Fund, Ethnic News Watch, Centers for Disease Control and Prevention.

Schools Get Results with Gun-Free Zones

Gloria Goodale

Special to
The Christian Science Monitor

RESEDA, CALIFORNIA—Reseda High School is fully armed. To fight against weapons on campus, that is. It is an official gun-free zone.

The site of one of the city's highly publicized student shootings in 1993, in which one teen deliberately killed another in the hallway, the San Fernando Valley campus has since become a virtual encyclopedia of programs to fight campus violence.

"For starters, we have a full-time Los Angeles police officer, in the nation's only specially adapted campus golf cart," says principal Bob Gladifko, brandishing a list of 14 activities aimed at halting campus violence. "After the shooting," the administrator says, "we started a zero-tolerance pupil expulsion policy of up to a year, [and] put our LAPD officer in uniform."

And in an effort that has been echoed around the country, the school put students at the center of many of its prevention programs, involving them in everything from peer counseling to clueing in adults to potential problems and weapons on campus.

Crimes involving weapons are increasing faster than any other type of juvenile offense, according to the US Justice Department. In a recent survey conducted by the National School Boards Association (NSBA), 31 percent of the school districts nationwide reported implementing gun-free zones, but all in combination with as many as 30 categories of efforts aimed at reducing school violence.

"Our sense is that the problem . . . has increased," says Laurie Westley, assistant executive director of the NSBA. "All over the country, we're seeing more programs, more hardware, and more focus on how to keep kids safe at school."

Across southern California, school districts have spared no effort in fighting violence. The Los Angeles Unified School District (LAUSD) lists 10 separate programs that are designed to protect and educate students about weapons and violence. These include several bilingual parent-training series, conflict-resolution programs, and STAR, or Straight Talk About Risks, an anti-weapons and violence program also found as far away as New York City public schools.

No district is immune. Even in relatively suburban areas, schools are getting tough in their fight against guns. Chatsworth High School, as well as the entire San Diego district, recently eliminated lockers from secondary schools to reduce the availability of drugs and weapons. Diamond Bar High School has implemented routine, random canine searches, using gunpowder-detecting dogs on campus.

Also in response to the 1993 shootings, LAUSD mandated daily, random metal screenings on all high school campuses. These are conducted by school administration personnel, but LAUSD police officers may be present. Larry Hutchens, assistant chief of the LAUSD school police, says this is for a good reason. "Visibility is an important issue," he says, adding, "Our very presence is a deterrent."

Officials at Reseda agree. In the wake of the Reseda shooting and another accidental shooting death at Fairfax High School in the same year, the school hired its police officer and began the expulsion policy in response to policy recommendations by the LAUSD.

But a crucial element in its prevention program has been WARN (Weapons Are Removed Now). The idea of Reseda teacher Jay Shaffer, WARN has been copied in districts from Baltimore, Maryland, to Pocatello, Idaho. Armed with the knowledge that students knew the gun was on campus the day of the shooting, Mr. Shaffer recruited student volunteers. "Kids are the first to know if a weapon is on campus," he observes, adding that his program is designed to get students to speak out.

The key? "Get them beyond their fear of retaliation," he says. "We use older kids to educate the younger kids that it's protecting everyone to speak out."

Indeed, recruiting students in the fight against violence has been a major factor in turning the tide, Mr. Gladifko says. Student participation is the common thread running through most Reseda programs, such as a suicide-prevention student-counseling strategy called IMPACT, a peer counseling program, a dress code, and an antiweapons contract signed by students, parents, and administrators.

"No one single program is responsible for turning the tide against violence. All these things work together," Gladifko explains, including a confidential tip line run by the district and a neighborhood school watch program.

Senior Tina London has been active in WARN for three years. The blond cheerleader says attitudes are changing. "Everybody realizes what's happening now. We want to stop the violence with our generation."

Deterrence is key, Gladifko says, noting that even private schools have joined the fight. His WARN group is scheduled to speak at a parochial high school following an incident there in which the principal was shot in the face by a student. Gladifko observes that violence at Reseda High has gone down since the 1993 shooting, and he recently asked parents at a community meeting whether the school should drop the metal screenings, since "we never find anything." The parents voted to keep the screenings "strictly for their value as a deterrent."

Gladifko observes: "We've created an island of safety," noting that "students are safer here than they are walking home."

"Now," he adds, "the community is next."

It was two minutes before the end of lunch, on a Friday. Students shuffled out of the cafeteria and ambled toward their fifth-period classes.

Suddenly, shots exploded outside. Then, gunfire ripped through the first-floor hallway. Everyone started running. The PA system blared out orders. Teachers herded students into classrooms and bolted the doors.

No one knew the specifics, but everyone knew what had happened. It was another shooting. Probably gang-related. And once again, the quietude of this neighborhood high school—one of the "safest" schools in Miami—had been blasted wide-open.

An eleventh-grade teacher (let's call her Mrs. Z) tried to present a calm exterior. She asked her students to sit down as usual and started them out on an informal vocabulary game. Meanwhile, police cars, ambulances, helicopters, and security officers with cell phones closed in on the school.

Finally, some students came running into Mrs. Z's classroom with the details: two students had been shot multiple times. They were seriously wounded.

A girl in the class looked up at Mrs. Z and said, "We should pray! We should pray for those kids who were shot!"

"That's a good idea," Mrs. Z said. "We can't do it as a class, though. It's against the law in Florida. But you can sure pray on your own. Matter of fact, I encourage you to pray."

So, as the class went on playing the vocabulary game—and as sirens and loudspeakers and helicopters filled the air with bedlam—students prayed, each one, individually. They prayed silently, in their hearts. And Mrs. Z prayed, too.

Of course, Mrs. Z doesn't know exactly what thoughts her students had as they prayed. But she did know they were praying, because they stopped acting scared. A feeling of calm settled down on the classroom.

School Shootings— and Individual Prayer

Mary Metzner Trammell

Associate Editor
Christian Science Sentinel

Mrs. Z knows how she prayed, though. It wasn't anything complicated. Mainly, she just remembered that God was there. Because He's everywhere. He was with her. He was with her class and with everybody else at the school. He was with the students who'd been shot. And always, always, God defends the innocent.

Just knowing these things made Mrs. Z feel more calm on the inside—not just acting calm on the outside. It made her feel God had already answered her prayers, and those of her students. And it actually made her feel safe, as if she and all the students at the school—even those who'd been shot—were in a secret, protected place where they couldn't be hurt.

Now, maybe you're wondering if there really is some secret place you can escape to when you're in danger. Or was Mrs. Z just imagining this feeling? Well, according to the Bible, there is such a place. "He that dwelleth in the secret place of the most High shall abide under the shadow of the Almighty," says the book of Psalms (91:1).

So where is this place? Actually, it's right where you are. It's in your thoughts. It's a place you can go to instantly by thinking of God—and His insuperable love and power and absolute goodness.

Maybe that sounds a little abstract. Maybe you're not sure you even believe in God. Or maybe you sometimes ask yourself why He allows things like shootings and gang wars to go on in the first place.

But is it really fair to blame God for things like this—things He never, ever would cause? Columnist Mike Barnicle of *The Boston Globe* thinks the answer to this question is a definite "NO." "God is not some sick, homicidal maniac," he wrote after a recent plane crash. "God does not play games with our lives. God's 'plan' doesn't involve explosives, bullets and bloodshed."[1]

We believe Barnicle is right. God is too perfectly good to cause evil. He doesn't cause teenagers to shoot teenagers. He doesn't cause the hopelessness and poverty and hatred that, experts say, drive teenagers to gangs and violence. He doesn't cause the juvenile violence that's "skyrocketing" in the United States.[2] And He doesn't cause what experts call the "new undergraduate class of ruthlessly violent teenagers who strike with abandon, indiscriminately and without remorse."[3]

Some people say these evils are products of our society. And that they'll continue indefinitely—because human nature itself is so hopelessly flawed.

But that reasoning just doesn't square with what God is and with what our nature really is. It doesn't square with God's absolute goodness and justice and love for every single one of us. What God is, makes us what we are. After all, we're His children. So we're not inherently evil. We're the effect of His perfectness. And so there's nothing more natural than for us to be good and just and loving—like God.

So, what does all this mean when there's a shooting in your city or your neighborhood? Or at your school? It means you have choices to make. You can choose not to do things that would only make the situation worse. For instance, you can choose not to panic. You can choose not to lose faith in God or humanity. You can choose not to get angry or vindictive.

And beyond that, you can choose to pray. You can opt to let good thoughts—thoughts about God's love and unfailing care for each one of His children—take over in your heart. You can take a stand for the basic redeemability of humanity. You can feel compassion toward people who mistakenly believe that violence is a legitimate way to express feelings or to prove how "tough" they are.

And you can do something more. You can find a faith in God's justice and mercy that assures you that good has to win out because God is omnipotent. And because—when you come right down to the truth of the matter—nothing besides God has any power at all.

Every thought like this helps. It helps save and heal the victims of crime. It helps you know what to do in a crisis. It protects you. And it takes a modest step toward redeeming teenage violence.

Astounding results can follow from your good, God-inspired thoughts—your constructive individual prayer. Mary Baker Eddy explained why. "Good thoughts are an impervious armor; clad therewith you are completely shielded from the attacks of error of every sort," she wrote. "And not only yourselves are safe, but all whom your thoughts rest upon are thereby benefited" (*The First Church of Christ, Scientist, and Miscellany*, p. 210).

That's what happened with the one-by-one prayers of Mrs. Z and her class. The students who had been shot improved rapidly. And everyone else felt able to return to school the following Monday.

True, there was talk of various countermeasures to stop future shootings—security guards, metal detectors, and such. But the previous Friday, some people at that school had learned about a more potent kind of countermeasure. They'd learned about how to enter, each one, into a "secret place" of prayer. A place that's hidden from danger. But even more than that, a place where God's love eliminates even the possibility of danger.

---

1 Mike Barnicle, "What does He make of it all?" *The Boston Globe*, July 25, 1996.
2 Jonathan Freedland, "Crime statistics show violence down in traditional American big-city areas," *The Ottawa Citizen*, December 6, 1994.　3 *The Trends Journal*, Fall 1995.

Chapter 4

Dealing

with the Media and Its Messages

Battles Over Media Violence Move to a New Frontier: The Internet

Gloria Goodale

**Special to
The Christian Science Monitor**

LOS ANGELES—Recent victories were won by the battle-weary researchers and activists who have spent entire careers combating violence in the media. Their efforts produced the V-chip, the three-hour-a-week-rule (for mandated network children's programming), impending TV ratings, and two independent, multi-year studies that for the first time have the support of both network and cable-TV producers. New anti–media violence programs also debuted at both the American Medical Association and the National Council of Churches.

But, like creeping shadows in a horror film, the explosion of new technologies such as the Internet and interactive video games is threatening to darken this victory parade with entirely new and, many say, more daunting challenges.

"The technology is going from passive to active," notes Professor Brian Stonehill, who created the media studies program at Pomona College in Claremont, California. "The violence is no longer vicarious with interactive media. It's much more pernicious and worrisome. Will we take responsibility for the thrill-seeking areas of our culture? That's what we're wrangling with now," he adds.

Technology always moves ahead of society's moral and ethical judgments, giving rise to a cultural lag, observes Richard Gelles, director of the Family Violence Research Program at the University of Rhode Island, in Kingston. While many people still can't afford the expensive new hardware and software (the average cost of a new computer setup is about $2,000 and video game decks average $200), Mr. Gelles says society must move on to consider the new issue. "The TV wars are over. The new wars are going to be brutal."

While years of research gave rise to the successes of the past year, work in the new areas is just beginning. Many scholars who might be expected to lead the charge are slow on the uptake. "I'm overwhelmed by the Internet," says Jeff Cole, lead author on the three-year network-funded study of television violence at UCLA's Center for Communication Policy. At the same time, he acknowledges, "It's the next frontier for everything."

Researchers, however, are not at ground zero. Much of what they now know about the impact of violence and how to handle it applies to these new technologies as well. For starters, the underlying assumptions about the effects of violence are no longer debated by most scholars. They are:

- Television violence can lead to imitation.
- Witnessing repeated violent acts can lead to desensitization and a lack of empathy for human suffering.
- The cumulative impact of violence-laden imagery can lead to a "mean-world" perspective, in which viewers have an unrealistically dark view of life.

Next, says UCLA's Mr. Cole, progress has been made in influencing the producers of material, in his case the networks. In undertaking yet another study in a field littered with reports, Cole's group was anxious to produce one that would make a difference.

They took a qualitative or contextual approach to analyzing the violence in network shows. In an area that has long been dominated by quantitative scholarship, Cole's is the largest qualitative study ever done. "We wanted to do something that was accessible to the public, so that when we write about a show like 'America's Funniest Home Videos,' we explain why."

The approach seems to have paid off. The UCLA report, which issued the second of three annual parts in September, noted that violence decreased from 1995 in several areas, notably in on-air promotions and movies of the week. Martin Franks, senior vice president at CBS, Inc. confirms that, in contrast to many other studies over the years, the UCLA study "gets referred to a lot. It sits on an awful lot of desks at CBS."

Ed Donnerstein, director of research for a big 1996 report, "The National Television Violence Study" (NTVS), funded by the cable industry, is less sanguine. Noting that the UCLA study was extremely selective, targeting only prime-time shows, the NTVS took a random sampling of a week's worth of programming. "We found that a good deal of violence goes unpunished, the pain or harm is unrealistic, and if someone gets hurt, it has no bearing on real life," he says.

But Mr. Donnerstein does acknowledge that both studies show an important sea-change in attitude. "At last, we're getting the producers of content to admit there's an issue," he notes, adding that the next step, namely, TV ratings due in January, may be the best indication of a real change. "At least there's a step here, given that nothing has moved for years."

Indeed, lessons gleaned from both the new TV ratings system, and blocking technologies such as the V-chip that are based on it, are already being applied to the Internet. The company that produced a ratings system for video games, the Recreational Software Advisory Council (RSAC), has created a similar system for sites on the Internet.

Many adults have long felt helpless to shelter children from pervasive media violence and sexual imagery. But after years of research and

How Much Do the Media Influence Children?

The Adults' View

The following survey is based on a poll of 1,209 adults, all of whom have kids aged 2 to 17 living with them.

How much do portrayals of sex in popular culture contribute to whether teenagers are sexually active?	A lot: 52% Little: 4% Some: 25% None: 17%
How much do portrayals of violence in popular culture contribute to whether teenagers are violent?	A lot: 56% Little: 5% Some: 26% None: 11%
Have you ever forbidden your child to see or listen to a particular television program, movie, or musical recording because you objected to the content?	TV Yes: 84% No: 16% Movie Yes: 64% No: 36% Music Yes: 42% No: 57%
What do you think is most to blame for teenage violence? The top five causes cited by all adults.	Television: 21% Lack of supervision: 13% Parents, unspecified: 8% Breakdown of family: 8% Drugs: 7%

Source: *The New York Times*

A telephone survey of 750 children ages 10 to 16 throughout the country on how television affects them.

The media are a significant influence:

66% say their peers are influenced by TV shows.

65% say shows like "The Simpsons" and "Married With Children" encourage kids to disrespect parents.

Sexual behavior on TV can sway kids' actions:

62% say that sex on TV shows and movies influences kids to have sex when they are too young.

77% say there is too much sex before marriage on television.

Kids say they get mixed messages about morals from watching TV shows:

49% think people are mostly dishonest.

54% say people care more about money than others.

46% say people are selfish.

51% say kids talk back to parents.

54% see people taking responsibility for their actions.

61% say people have generally good morals.

Viewing habits change when parents aren't around:

55% watch TV alone or with friends, not with family.

44% watch something different when they're alone than with their parents (25% choose MTV).

54% have a TV in their bedroom.

Source: Fairbank, Maslin, Maullin & Associates

activism, the tide is shifting toward better programming and ratings systems, particularly on TV. As those battles subside, a new challenge is forming with the vast world of the Internet.

Joel Federman is codirector of the Center for Communication and Social Policy at the University of California at Santa Barbara. He notes that several major companies such as Microsoft and CompuServe already have announced they will use the RSAC ratings. Once the sites are rated, consumers can use a Web-blocking device that will access only the sites with desirable ratings. Unrated sites can also be blocked.

Federman says that, although some technologies are being developed to help parents deal with violent or otherwise unacceptable material such as pornography on the Internet, the biggest problem may be a technology gap between generations. "Parents may not understand enough about the technology to really effectively protect their kids." However, this doesn't absolve parents of the most basic responsibility implicit in all the research. Says Professor Stonehill: "We have to sort and choose as a culture. It's a bumpy path, but it's still up to us."

Just as researchers have generally agreed on the effects of violence, they've also narrowed down the sort of children most at risk to be adversely influenced. Not surprisingly, the unsupervised child is high on the list.

BOSTON—Like many parents, Sarah Woodruff is concerned about the messages and images her children see in the media. So when she took her sons, ages 4 and 6, to see the movie *Fly Away Home* in Durham, North Carolina, she didn't foresee any problems. But then came the previews—along with Barbara Streisand screaming that she wanted sex, now. "I was cringing. I was angry," Ms. Woodruff recalls. "How come nobody thought this would be inappropriate for young children?"

Experiences like Woodruff's resonate with many parents. The media's long reach has made it difficult to shield children from messages some consider inappropriate or negative.

From car crashes and sex scenes to glamorizing drugs and hypermarketing, the effect of media images on children has caused concern for decades. Violence has raised particular ire, and for good reason: The average child viewer will see 20,000 murders and 80,000 other assaults before leaving elementary school.

But in the past several years, a groundswell of activity has grown not only to monitor media messages but to respond to and influence them.

Parents are sending protest letters to entertainment executives and analyzing TV shows with their children. Media literacy groups, as well as family and religious organizations, are offering education and ratings. Many state medical associations are labeling media violence a public-health issue and launching campaigns to combat it.

"The change is in the level of awareness," says David Walsh, director of the National Institute on Media and the Family in Minneapolis. Every time a major survey comes out, the percentage of parents who say they are concerned about the negative influence of media on children goes up. But how they're responding is changing. In 1994, for example, Dr. Walsh published *Selling Out America's Children:*

More Parents Turn to an Old-Fashioned V-Chip: Themselves

Kirsten A. Conover

Staff Writer
The Christian Science Monitor

How America Puts Profits Before Values and What Parents Can Do.
What prompted him to write the book was the word "it."

"I kept hearing that word in the late '80s and '90s wherever I went," says Walsh, who conducts seminars on the subject. Parents would say things like, "There's nothing we can do about it, it is such a powerful force. I feel like we're just overmatched by it." A major part of what "it" is, he says, is mass media that influence attitudes and, in turn, values.

The most pivotal issue has been media violence. Politicians have leaned on Hollywood in response to public pressure, and gotten results: V-chip legislation has brought the discussion to the fore. Networks have been told to provide three hours per week of children's programming and to rate all their shows starting in 1997.

Why? Children and teenagers spend 22 to 28 hours a week watching TV; the only thing they do more of is sleep. Prime-time viewers see an average of 150 acts of violence and about 15 murders a week.

Close to 65 percent of parents report that they limit their children's viewing time. But they can't always control what kids see.

Just ask Diane Levin. She and her family were on an airplane delayed for take-off. The Florida-bound plane was full of families. For their "viewing pleasure," they were shown a short news summary—of mass murders. "It's showing bodies, and it's showing people crying. . . ." she recalls. Ms. Levin called a flight attendant. "Get that off," she said. "That's outrageous, there are kids on this plane." By the time they did, the show had ended.

But officials apologized and wrote it up on the flight report. "One voice can make a difference," says Levin, a professor at Wheelock College in Boston. She finds herself saying that a lot. A child-development expert, Levin has done much research and written several books on media violence and war toys and their influence on children.

A year and a half ago, she founded Teachers for Resisting Unhealthy Children's Entertainment (TRUCE), a Somerville, Massachusetts, group of educators and parents. TRUCE members encourage adults to write a letter or make a phone call every week expressing disapproval or approval of what they see in the media, on the Internet, and in the marketplace. "It seems like we're reaching a critical mass, and it's about to take off," Levin says.

TRUCE is one of many such groups sprouting up around the country. "We found just in the past year a greater receptivity in the industry to thinking about the ramifications of what they're showing," says Laurie

Trotta, director of communications for Mediascope, a nonprofit public policy group in Studio City, California. She attributes such progress to "political and social forces."

In Bethesda, Maryland, the Lion & Lamb Project aims to stop the merchandising of violence to children. "For a while, there was this sense that [parents] were helpless against the barrage," says founder and executive director Daphne White. "But now they're recognizing that they do have power over their children's entertainment choices."

At the same time, national groups have raised their profile. The American Family Association, based in Tupelo, Miss., is leading a boycott of the Disney Corp. They charge that Disney has "slid into the gutter" with violent movies such as *Pulp Fiction* and what they call antifamily values in films aimed at younger audiences. Another project of the Christian group is its drive to get "trash talk" TV shows off the air.

Americans for Responsible Television in Bloomfield Hills, Michigan, is also working to better the offerings by contacting advertisers who sponsor programs.

A survey released by the American Medical Association in September, 1996 stated that 75 percent of parents are "disgusted" with media violence, and that parents overwhelmingly want stronger rating systems for movies, television shows, and computer games.

"Parents want more information on the negative as well as the positive," says David Walsh of the National Institute on Media and the Family. The Institute recently announced plans to produce its own rating system for all media products.

Indeed, nothing can substitute for what goes on in the home, says Walsh. He, like many experts, is emphatic about keeping televisions out of kids' bedrooms. He counsels parents to watch TV only when something good is on. Parents also must inform themselves about what their kids are watching and playing on the screen.

Another key issue is media literacy. The movement has gained ground in helping families understand the media and the way TV, for example, delivers "eyeballs to advertisers." If viewers are more savvy, the reasoning goes, they will be less likely to be manipulated.

"We need to instill and establish ways to deal with media in the lives of children and in raising our children in the 21st century," says Elizabeth Thoman, founder and executive director of the Center for Media Literacy in Los Angeles. How? Manage viewing, have schools teach critical viewing skills, and participate in larger public debates.

Reinforcement may also come from religious groups. The National Council of Churches has deemed 1997 "Media Awareness Year." The focal point will be a national teleconference in May on media issues from consumerism to substance abuse.

Cathi Coridan is a youth minister and a media-literacy consultant. "People are beginning to understand that popular culture is not something that happens to us, it's something we create," she says. "Just as parents buckle their kids in [the car], they need to start doing other things to safeguard their children."

BOSTON — "Media violence has hit a deep emotional wellspring in society," says Renee Hobbs, a media literacy expert. "It is the topic around which the fields of media literacy and television have been defined."

This night, Ms. Hobbs is giving a seminar to a roomful of educators, ranging from school teachers and administrators to the local D.A.R.E. officer in Yarmouth, Massachusetts. The talk is titled "Beyond Blame: Challenging Violence in the Media," a resource program created by the Center for Media Literacy in Los Angeles.

Ms. Hobbs focuses on what she calls a "circle of blame." It goes something like this: Parents blame producers; producers blame viewers for wanting to watch violent shows; and Congress points to the First Amendment as a reason it can't restrict TV violence. "The status quo has been really comfortable blaming someone else," Hobbs says.

One main push of media literacy is to understand the impact of violence on the media's bottom line: It sells and travels well.

"Our goal is to change the way we watch," Hobbs says. Analytical, critical viewing includes challenging what you see and hear, deconstructing messages, asking questions, and discussing.

For example, after showing clips of television and movie violence, Hobbs distributes a handout with questions a parent or teacher might ask children. Who gets hurt? Do you think this happens in real life? Why do you suppose the producers used that kind of music? With teenagers, discussions are more involved. How are men and women portrayed in violent movies? Watch the evening news for a week and see if you detect the assumption: "If it bleeds, it leads."

Noting the effects of media violence, Hobbs cites the following findings of the American Psychological Association's (APA) Commission on Violence and Youth:

Beyond Blame: Media Literacy at Work

Kirsten A. Conover

Staff Writer
The Christian Science Monitor

- Aggressor effect. Attitudes of accepting violence sometimes lead to aggressive behavior.
- Victim effect. (The "mean world" syndrome.) Watching excessive amounts of violence can cause people to think their communities are more dangerous than they really are.
- Bystander effect. Desensitization, a callousness toward violence, can result in less likelihood to take action on behalf of victims.
- Appetite effect. Viewers crave increasingly violent material to remain stimulated.

Education and resensitization through parental guidance and awareness can help counter such effects.

Superseding the Hollywood "Ministry of Culture"

Gloria Goodale

**Special to
The Christian Science Monitor**

LOS ANGELES—George Gerbner has a tale to tell, about a community of people who've lost their stories and the forces he says have taken them away. It is about all of us and the international media empire Mr. Gerbner calls the "invisible, unelected, unaccountable, private Ministry of Culture making decisions that shape public policy behind closed doors."

Dean of the University of Pennsylvania's Annenberg School for Communication from 1964 to 1989, Gerbner is the undisputed granddaddy of research into the effects of media images on all of us.

His response to the problems of violent or otherwise harmful media imagery is not to "rearrange the window dressing," but to foment a revolution. "The problem is the system," muses the author of articles with titles like "Invisible Crises: What Conglomerate Media Control Means for America and the World."

"The total cultural environment is an appendage of a marketing apparatus, produced to market other goods," Gerbner explains. He says violence in the media is simply a demonstration of power—who can get away with what.

Gerbner's answer: the Cultural Environment Movement (CEM), a coalition of more than 150 groups and activists in the United States and 63 other countries on six continents. CEM kicked off with a founding convention in St. Louis this past March and has as its lofty goal to move people to "take control of their cultural environment and shape it to meet human needs."

With this movement, Gerbner hopes to empower people to reject what he calls a homogenized, Hollywood-produced culture in favor of local, individualized stories. CEM's 25-point agenda calls for a CEM action day, a Global Marketing Awareness Task Force, media-literacy programs in churches and schools, ad-free zones for schools, and the establishment of a National Endowment for Telecommunications to find alternatives to commercial advertising.

Brian Stonehill, who founded the media-literacy program at Pomona College in Claremont, California, attended the CEM convention and likens it to the environmental movement. "In the beginning, it seemed radical and people called them all tree-huggers. But look how quickly the ideas have moved into our mainstream," he adds, observing that now we take efforts like recycling paper for granted.

Mr. Stonehill says Gerbner's movement is designed to wake people up. "This whole debate will be useful if it goes beyond simulations [such as television] to the ways in which we actually treat each other," he says.

Having spent a lifetime studying media violence, Gerbner is impatient with the politicization of the issue, but says it all boils down to one simple message: "We need people with stories to tell, not things to sell."

A New Approach to Education: For the Safety of Children

Barbara M. Vining

Associate Editor
The Christian Science Journal

How can society most effectively combat the evils that threaten the development, safety, and health of children? Could it be that certain strengths lying within children themselves deserve to be more widely recognized—and that drawing out these strengths should be our aim in the education and defense of children? There are encouraging signs that point in this direction.

One example of someone who has found a way to help bring out the inherent strengths of children is Valerie Hamilton, a physical education teacher. Violence—including the murder of students she had taught, and the murder of parents of students—propelled her into action. Through summer camps, motivational programs, and a publication for youth called *Star Child Affairs Magazine*, she is helping children find the strength within themselves to say no to drugs, gangs, and other self-destructive behaviors. All her efforts are aimed at preventing violence in the lives of young people. A seven-year-old reader of her magazine says, "Once you learn the difference between good and bad, it will be a lot better."[1]

Some years ago, when our own children were growing up, a business associate of my husband's joined our family at dinner one night. There was something about his natural appreciation of children that brought out the very best in them. They blossomed in his presence. During this gentle man's hour or two in our home, I saw beautiful qualities in our children that I had barely perceived before. I learned a valuable lesson in how to bring out what is already present in every child, in fact in everyone.

It has rightly been said—and the above instances clearly indicate—that true education is not a pouring in but a drawing out. It is the bringing out of possibilities already within us, within every child, man, and woman. And one of the most valuable things we all have within us is the ability to know right from wrong—to be good and to do good. This ability comes to us from God; moral and spiritual strength are intrinsic to our true being as children of God, Spirit, as His spiritual image and likeness. As such, they are inseparable from God and are maintained and sustained by Him alone. They are neither dependent upon nor subject to anything other than God.

Christ Jesus certainly appreciated the value and spiritual strength of children. When the people sought to bring children to Jesus to receive his blessing, and his "disciples rebuked them" because they didn't want the Master to be interrupted in his work, Jesus said: "Suffer little children, and forbid them not, to come unto me: for of such is the kingdom of heaven. And he laid his hands on them, and departed thence."[2]

Doesn't Jesus' love for children point to the need we each have to cherish the childlike qualities within ourselves—the pure, God-derived elements of thought most often associated with children? Doing so, we'll help to bring out naturally the strengths in our children and ourselves. Through a Christlike appreciation and perception of every child, and of one another, we'll also help to destroy any abusive tendencies, any carnal elements of thought, that would crush out innocence and purity in the human family. We can't abuse what we truly cherish as inherent in our being as a child of God.

Children would surely have blossomed from within in the presence of Jesus because of the Christ, Truth, which he embodied and expressed as the Son of God—because of the spiritual purity he radiated. This same Truth is here today for us to embody and express in our own hearts and lives. And we have within ourselves, as does every child, the ability to profit from the ever-present influence of Truth in human consciousness, and to blossom. As we trust God and His Christ to guide us, our moral and spiritual strengths develop steadily. Moral strength has to do with the willingness to distinguish between right and wrong and to behave rightly in every aspect of our lives, including in our relations with others. Spiritual strength has to do with expressing the spiritual qualities we possess and reflect from God by reason of our inseparable relation to Him as His likeness.

Above all else, the education of children—at home, at school, and through the media, as well as at Sunday School—should draw out their inherent moral and spiritual strengths. *Science and Health with Key to the Scriptures* by Mary Baker Eddy affirms, "The entire education of children should be such as to form habits of obedience to the moral and spiritual law, with which the child can meet and master the belief in so-called physical laws, a belief which breeds disease."[3]

Yes, the moral and spiritual development of children is crucial to their well-being, not only for their social and educational development, but for their safety and their health—and for the safety and health of society as well. And the more we cherish our own pure, childlike qualities, the more we'll be supporting this development, bringing out what is inherent in all children as well as in ourselves. "The belief in so-called physical laws" is the breeding ground of disease—mental, physical, social; and it also breeds violence. But it is proved powerless through "obedience to the moral and spiritual law." And it is natural for each of us to love and obey this law.

One time, I took a class in how to teach phonics reading to children and adults. The teacher of this class had widely acclaimed success with the method she taught, which included bits of wisdom that reached far beyond the academic development of children. One day in class she illustrated her conviction that corrections in behavior in a classroom should come from within a child whenever possible, rather than from embarrassing personal rebuke. During the course of teaching, she suddenly stopped and quietly, but firmly, said, "I see impatience in the classroom." I remember well my own response: I silently examined my thinking to see if I could possibly be the one she was referring to. After a moment or two of obvious self-examination and self-correction throughout the classroom, she resumed teaching. Impatience having been identified as undesirable in her classroom, we each saw to it that it did not come up again.

God alone is law to His creation. Through obedience to God and His laws, any individual can become a law to himself or herself. According to the demonstrable spiritual law of being, each of us forever exists as the formation and expression of God, Mind, not matter. And we are all forever governed and protected by divine Mind. This truth is powerful to remove violence both from individual lives and from society.

As we deeply realize in prayer Mind's government of its offspring, and yield to this government in our lives, we'll be taking an active part in a new approach to education that helps to bring out the full potential of the inner strengths already within every child. This is crucial in ridding society of the evils that threaten children. Through our prayers, our genuine love for children, and our growing love of the childlike qualities we all express, we will see more clearly God's care for all His offspring. Children will find their God-given strengths being naturally drawn out. And we all will find real safety and healing in Truth's embrace.

---

1 *The Boston Globe*, May 13, 1996.   2 Matthew 19:13–15.   3 *Science and Health*, p. 62.

Chapter 5

5

Protecting
Children from Internet
Dangers

"Off-Line" Hazards Lie in Web's Links, Lures

Mark Clayton

Staff Writer
The Christian Science Monitor

TORONTO—The Orchid Club was once a lurid corner on the information superhighway—an Internet conference room or "chat room" where members thousands of miles apart could meet in cyberspace and trade homemade child pornography, both in words and pictures.

To enter the club's electronic backroom, members needed a password. No one could join the club without a referral from a member, and initiates were required to send other members a description of a sexual encounter with a child.

According to a federal indictment in San Jose, California, Orchid Club members used an on-line electronic medium known as "Internet relay chat," or IRC, to not only share live conversations but also to transmit digitized still pictures and live video images of children as they were being molested by a member.

The Orchid Club was exposed in July of 1996 after police began investigating the sexual abuse of a six-year-old girl in Greenfield, California. Federal indictments list the names of 16 Orchid Club members in the United States, Canada, Finland, and Australia on charges of conspiring to produce and disseminate child pornography.

But the Orchid Club's members were hardly alone in their peculiar use of the Internet.

Internet Porn as Threat

As home access to the Internet grows rapidly, so too does the threat that this on-line medium will expand opportunities for sexual exploitation of children—particularly in United States and Canada where sales of home PCs are booming.

About 10 million people use on-line services and tens of millions more use the Internet worldwide—including IRC and the graphics-oriented World Wide

Web. Among those millions, a small percentage are pedophiles who discover each other in unregulated electronic forums. They typically exchange experiences and pictures, police say, which then reinforces their behavior and encourages more physical encounters with children "off-line."

The Internet's role in facilitating a renewed spate of child sexual exploitation has ignited furious debate in Europe, the United States, and Canada over free-speech rights and government regulation of a new communications medium as untamed as the old American Wild West.

In the case of the Orchid Club, children were not apparently molested for profit. But sexual abuse was encouraged by the conferencing ability of the Internet. And it is only a click of a computer mouse from that kind of chat room to a normal kids' chat room, police say.

Pedophilia Expands Reach

While it is certainly possible for technically adept kids to find child pornography on their own on the Internet, the key danger of child sexual exploitation is significantly more subtle.

Given the anonymity that is possible on the Internet, an increasing number of pedophiles are feigning youth in their electronic personae as they troll through various forums looking for children to abuse. Often this does not require even getting on the Internet directly, but onto the side-roads of an on-line "brand" service.

Few police departments have specialists focusing on computer on-line exploitation of children. But as the problem grows, so do calls for more attention to it. Douglas Rehman, a special agent of the Florida Department of Law Enforcement, has made 12 arrests over two years of people using the Internet either for child porn or to meet kids to have sex with them. "This is not a static percentage—it's a growth crime," Mr. Rehman says. "The Internet and on-line services are the absolute best hunting ground the pedophile could wish for."

Nationwide, he estimates 250–300 charges of child sexual exploitation using the Internet have been brought in the last two years. Typically a child uses the family computer to dial onto the Internet through a service provider or onto one of the on-line services, all of which have electronic "forums" set aside for children. During these instantaneous on-line electronic chat sessions, children send electronic messages to other kids who appear to have common interests.

But because there is near anonymity, it is impossible for a child to know if the person named "Terri" with whom he or she is communicating is a 12-year-old girl or a 45-year-old man pretending to be a young girl. On-line services now provide adult "hosts" to keep an eye on discussions and watch for abuses. But IRC chat groups and Internet newsgroups designated with "alt." prefix in the Internet address usually have no such regulation.

The Child Who Isn't

Pretending to be a child, the pedophile may converse with a real child in an open chat forum. But it may be a short step thereafter into a "private" one-on-one chat room, police say. At that point, a pedophile will use different questions and techniques to discover a child's vulnerabilities. Do they have disagreements with their parents? Do they like to party? Do they like pornography? Drugs?

A pedophile often will eventually send pictures of pornography from his computer to the child's computer in hopes of "lowering the child's inhibitions," toward having sex, police say. What may follow then will be a suggestion that the two actually meet. The child may not know until the moment of the meeting that his 12-year-old electronic pen pal is actually a man.

But anonymity works both ways. A former volunteer at several local youth groups in Uxbridge, Massachusetts, was arrested on federal charges that he used an on-line computer service to solicit sex from a youth he thought was under 18. Police say the man traveled to Troy, New York, believing he would be meeting a 13-year-old boy for a sexual encounter.

In fact, the "boy" was a reporter from an Albany, New York, television station who had arranged the meeting after finding a solicitation for sex in one of the chat rooms of the America Online service last year.

One professional cybercop is Toby Tyler, who surfs the Net from his computer terminal in the San Bernadino (California) County Sheriff's Department. He searches for scams, sources of child porn, and deceptions designed to entrap children. Five investigators in his department are busy full-time investigating child sexual exploitation—much of it flowing from pedophiles trying to set up meetings with children by computer.

The Internet is a "two-edged sword" for child pornographers, Deputy Tyler says. On the one hand, he says, it seems to have damaged the profitability of pornographers who sell their wares via dial-up computer "bulletin board." There is so much free stuff on the Internet—why would anyone pay? On the other hand, wide access to child pornography may be building an appetite among pedophiles that could lead to more children being molested and a wider market and profit for the child pornographer.

Child pornography was nearly stamped out as a cottage industry in the United States in the 1980s, but has resurged in the 1990s in unregulated Internet news groups, "chat rooms," and commercial on-line services. Today child pornography that was produced, mostly in Scandinavian countries in the 1960s, '70s, and early '80s, is being scanned or digitized and re-released on CD-ROMs advertised to a global audience on the Internet.

"The ability to mass market child pornography with little or no overhead to huge populations has created an environment where pressures for new material exist," says Kevin V. Di Gregory, deputy assistant attorney general in the United States Justice Department in June testimony before Congress. "This demand, unfortunately, is being met by new material from sources which include the Pacific Rim countries . . . ."

On the technological cutting edge of child pornography lurks a practice in which graphics software can splice any child's picture into a pornographic image to create a fictional scene that never occurred. The danger is that such images might be used to coerce or blackmail children into silence—or to seduce them.

Mr. Di Gregory says the Justice Department wants Congress to ban such computer-altered images on the same legal basis that child pornography is banned, namely, damage to the individual child.

There are already reports, however, of at least one site on the Web where a pornographic image of a computer-generated "virtual child"—who does not exist but looks lifelike—is displayed. Under current laws, such "child pornography" would be difficult or impossible to prosecute.

Until society has agreed on better ways to end child pornography on the Internet, police say parents or schools will have to closely monitor the use of the Internet by children.

"We warn our kids about strangers," Rehman, the special agent in Florida, says. "We're not as attentive when they're sitting at home, comfortable and safe, and the door is locked. But the stranger that comes in through the [computer modem] is every bit as dangerous."

For parents a few mouse-clicks behind their kids on the Internet, help has arrived: software baby-gates.

These blocking or filtering devices help prevent children from falling prey to any nasty spiders on the Internet's World Wide Web.

Whether the dangers are indecent sites or electronic chat rooms with anonymous pedophiles, a whole industry is booming to help parents (and schools and libraries) guide children toward safe surfing.

The best advice for parents is to sit with their child at the computer and know what the Web offers in its galaxy of goodies and how a child is using it. Linking to the many fun and educational kid sites can temper the temptation to trip down dark alleys of the Web.

But like TV before it, the Web is ripe for some sort of regulation. Right now, the jury's still out on whether government, companies, or parents—or all three—will do the regulating.

National on-line-service providers, such as America Online and CompuServe, police their own electronic byways. And companies eager to fend off government regulation are rushing to set industry standards to help parents block access to dubious Web sites or to use rating systems to judge content.

Netscape, Microsoft, and other companies have put their stamp of approval on just such an emerging standard, called Platform for Internet Content Selection (PICS), as a filter system for site selection.

Here are some software programs to help parents guide a child's use of the Web:

- SurfWatch Software's SurfWatch
  800-458-6600
  http://www.surfwatch.com
- Cyber Patrol from Microsystems Software
  800-489-2001
  http://www.microsys.com

Safe Surfing: Ways to Guide a Child's Web Use

Staff
The Christian Science Monitor

- NewView Inc.'s Specs for Kids
  http://www.newview.com
- Solid Oak Software's CYBERSitter
  805-967-9853
  http://www.solidoak.com
- InterGo's KinderGuard
  972-424-7882
  http://www.intergo.com
- Trove Investment Corp.'s Net Nanny
  800-340-7177
  http://www.netnanny.com
- Turner Investigation, Research, and Communication and J.D. Koftinoff Software Ltd.'s Internet Filter (Canada, British Columbia)
  604-708-2397
  http://www.turnercom.com
- Net Shepherd Inc.'s daxHOUND (Canada, Alberta)
  403-218-8900
  http://www.netshepherd.net

Here are a few helpful sites that keep track of issues on the Web and children:

- SafeSurf
  http://www.safesurf.com
- Recreational Software Advisory Council
  http://www.rsac.org
- Project OPEN
  http://www.isa.net/project-open/empower.html
- Larry Magid's Kids Page
  http://www.larrysworld.com/kids.html
- SAFE-T-CHILD On-line
  http://www.yellodyno.com
- The Internet Advocate
  http://www.monroe.lib.in.us/~lchampel/netadv.html

Here are tips for both parents and children on how to safely use the Web. They were written by Lawrence J. Magid (author of *Cruising On-line: Larry Magid's Guide to the New Digital Highway*, Random House, 1994) for the National Center for Missing and Exploited Children (800-843-5678) and Interactive Services Association. An on-line version of these guidelines can be obtained from the ISA's Web site: http://www.isa.net/isa.

Some Rules of the Road for the Information Highway

Staff
The Christian Science Monitor

Guidelines for Parents

Never give out identifying information—home address, school name, or telephone number—in a public message such as chat or bulletin boards, and be sure you're dealing with someone that both you and your child know and trust before giving it out via e-mail. Think carefully before revealing any personal information such as age, marital status, or financial information. Consider using a pseudonym or unlisting your child's name if your service allows it.

Get to know the services your child uses. If you don't know how to log on, get your child to show you. Find out what types of information they offer and whether there are ways for parents to block out objectionable material.

Never allow a child to arrange a face-to-face meeting with another computer user without parental permission. If a meeting is arranged, make the first one in a public spot and be sure to accompany your child.

Never respond to messages or bulletin board items that are suggestive, obscene, belligerent, threatening, or make you feel uncomfortable. Encourage your children to tell you if they encounter such messages. If you or your child receives a message that is harassing, of a sexual nature, or threatening, forward a copy of the message to your service provider and ask for its assistance.

Report child pornography. Should you become aware of the transmission, use, or viewing of child pornography while on-line, immediately report this to the National Center for Missing and Exploited Children by calling 800-843-5678. You should also notify your on-line service provider.

Remember that people on-line may not be who they seem. Because you can't see or even hear the person, it would be easy for someone to misrepresent him—or herself. Thus, someone indicating that "she" is a "12-year-old girl" could in reality be a 40-year-old man.

Remember that not everything you read on-line is necessarily true. Any offer that's "too good to be true" probably is. Be very careful about any offers that involve your coming to a meeting or having someone visit your house.

Set reasonable rules and guidelines for computer use by your children. Discuss these rules and post them near the computer as a reminder. Remember to monitor their compliance with these rules, especially when it comes to the amount of time your children spend on the computer. A child or teenager's excessive use of on-line services or bulletin boards, especially late at night, may indicate a potential problem. Remember that personal computers and on-line services should not be used as electronic babysitters.

Make Internet computing a family activity. Consider keeping the computer in a family room rather than the child's bedroom. Get to know their "on-line friends" just as you get to know all of their other friends.

Children's Rules for On-line Safety

1. I will not give out personal information such as my address, telephone number, parents' work address/telephone number, or the name and location of my school without my parents' permission.
2. I will tell my parents right away if I come across any information that makes me feel uncomfortable.
3. I will never agree to get together with someone I "meet" on-line without first checking with my parents. If my parents agree to the meeting, I will be sure that it is in a public place and bring my mother or father along.

4. I will never send a person my picture or anything else without first checking with my parents.
5. I will not respond to any messages that are mean or in any way make me feel uncomfortable. It is not my fault if I get a message like that. If I do I will tell my parents right away so that they can contact the on-line service.
6. I will talk with my parents so that we can set up rules for going on-line. We will decide on the times of day that I can be on-line, the length of time I can be on-line, and appropriate areas for me to visit. I will not access other areas or break these rules without their permission.

Are you familiar with St. Paul's words in the Bible "...the carnal mind is enmity against God"? (Romans 8:7) This important statement exposes the nature of the hatred that leads to abuse of children, especially sexual abuse.

Those who entertain erotic fantasies about children are actually expressing hatred of innocence and purity. This destroys the natural pattern of trust between adults and children—a pattern that should reflect the relation of God to man.

If we have an interest in ending such abuse, we need to learn how to nullify and destroy the influence "the carnal mind" has over the thoughts and actions of people.

Some people who are ignorant of the true nature of God and His creation tend to think that hate, lust, passion, and greed are strong; and that love, purity, innocence, and goodness are weak and vulnerable. Yet the life of Christ Jesus, who knew God intimately, proves that the opposite is true.

Once a vengeful mob threw a woman, caught in the crime of adultery, in front of Jesus. But His goodness and purity worked strongly on their thoughts. His good qualities quenched a lust to kill exhibited by the mob and rebuked the behavior of the woman herself. Study of the Bible reveals Jesus to have done two things repeatedly in his ministry. First, he brought people face to face with their own thinking and character; and then he awakened within men and women their God-given ability to choose to be good.

Good is the manifestation of God's presence and power. It is not fragile. It is the bedrock of creation. The power of God, of divine good, gives men and women dominion over the apparent drives of the carnal mind. The more we learn of God's power and strength, the more, like Jesus, we will be able to prove that they reign in each one of us, despite evidence to the contrary.

74

Mary Baker Eddy, who discovered the laws of God she called Christian Science, wrote, "If thought is startled at the strong claim of Science for the supremacy of God, or Truth, and doubts the supremacy of good, ought we not, contrariwise, to be astounded at the vigorous claims of evil and doubt them, and no longer think it natural to love sin and unnatural to forsake it,—no longer imagine evil to be ever-present and good absent?" This is from *Science and Health with Key to the Scriptures* (p. 130). The book says further on, "The central fact of the Bible is the superiority of spiritual over physical power" (p. 131).

A realization of these facts enables us to grow in the ability to defend the community from the predatory activities of the carnal mind. The Science of Christianity, understood and practiced, exposes evil's hidden activities. It restrains crime. It neutralizes hatred and lust. It brings God's power to bear on human events.

Human behavior theories often excuse the carnal thoughts that lead to abuse, when these theories speculate that we are fallen, the victims of original sin, or when they suggest that genetics or psychological injuries have predisposed individuals to abusive behavior. Such admissions often leave men and women helpless to improve. But God's children are not the victims of sin or of genetic mutations. Jesus revealed, and the Science of Christ continues to demonstrate, that we are the work of God. We can follow Jesus' example and prove that God's Word rules in the heart. God's powerful message of salvation gives men and women the spiritual desire and power to conquer the domination of carnal desire. Prayer to God in behalf of children is one important means of delivering society from sin.

Those who want to pray specifically to rid their communities of abusive behavior can begin by striving to know more of the nature of God. The more we know of Him, the more we know of ourselves and the more we are effective in annulling the action of the carnal mind.

Our children will be safer when we realize that the carnal mind is not native to anyone, but is an aggressive imposition on the thought, something that spiritual understanding alone can and does destroy.

Chapter

6

Battling
the Child Sex Trade

Sex Trade Lures Kids from Burbs

Mark Clayton

Staff Writer
The Christian Science Monitor

VANCOUVER—Leslie is just over five feet tall. A bit unsteady on her white platform shoes, she stands up straight so the men gawking from their cars in this alley can get a good look at her.

Her face is that of an adolescent—young, round, unmarked by abuse. Her long maple-hued hair is held back by a white band that at a glance lends an angelic halo. She wears skin-tight white leotards and a white pullover.

Leslie is 14 years old. She began selling her body to the men prowling this area a year ago, after her 13th birthday. She is younger than many here, which makes Leslie a prized commodity on Vancouver's "kiddie stroll," a street in the warehouse district where men who want sex with young girls know they can find them. For those wanting young boys, "boys' town" is nearby.

"I usually just do two tricks a day," she tells a reporter who has stopped to talk with her. "I could make more money. But I'm really just working to buy what my parents can't pay for."

Why this work? Couldn't she be flipping burgers at McDonald's?

"Let's just say I would rather get paid for sex than be forced to do it for free anyway," she says. And then in just a few minutes, her tale of being sexually abused spills out. She was molested by a baby sitter when she was 4, raped at age 12 by a 17-year-old boy she knew. She was put in a Calgary foster home she hated, then ran back to her Vancouver family.

Working on the same corner with Leslie is her guardian angel, Tina. An 18-year-old string-bean of a girl with reddish-brown, shoulder-length hair, Tina wears John Lennon-style dark glasses, short shorts, a pullover, a black cap—and platform shoes.

Tina doesn't agree with Leslie's decision to be a prostitute. But she understands it. She, too, was once young and sexually abused at home. She also hit the streets believing it would give her independence and

78

power. Tina's illusion was broken after a pimp beat her senseless at age 15. She was then taken from Calgary to Seattle and traded among at least a half-dozen pimps thereafter. Now too wise to the pimp's game to be controlled by them, the only reason she prostitutes herself, she says, is to earn money to feed her baby.

"I tell her [Leslie] she shouldn't be out here," Tina says. "But she's like me when I was young. I didn't know anything then either. I thought this was the only way I could make it. I try to keep the pimps away from her every day. I tell them she works for me. But I worry about her."

At this moment, a gold Mercedes swings around the corner, an olive-complexioned man in sunglasses grinning at the wheel. Cruising by for perhaps the 10th time, he again yells something.

"Ugh, I hate that guy," Leslie says disgustedly. She resumes talking, saying she will be in the ninth grade this fall—but will still be engaged in prostitution after school and on weekends.

While US and Canadian lawmakers fulminate against "child sex tours" to places like Bangkok, few acknowledge the growing number of children bought, sold, and recruited into prostitution daily in cities across North America. Today in the US and Canada there are between 100,000 and 300,000 children under age 18 trapped in prostitution, researchers say. The average age of entry into prostitution is 14 years old. The vast majority of adult prostitutes say they entered prostitution before age 18.

Like children in Thailand, India, and elsewhere, most North American children enter prostitution not because they "choose" to, but because adults—pimps and customers—are expert at identifying and exploiting those that are vulnerable, child advocates say. Many children are running from sexual abuse at home, but end up finding more of it than they ever imagined on the streets.

The pimp's gold mine is more than 500,000 vulnerable children who run away or are "thrown away" (shut out of their homes) annually in the US, according to the National Center for Missing and Exploited Children in Arlington, Virginia.

Not all "street" children enter prostitution. The key factor that determines who will and who won't is sexual abuse at home. More than 80 percent of children who do enter the sex trade say they were sexually or physically abused at home.

Within 48 hours of hitting the streets, a juvenile will be approached with an offer of money, food, or shelter in exchange for sex. Many will rationalize this "survival sex." Often they are told this "work" will earn them big money and empower them. After all, they are told by pimps, "only a fool does it for free. And you were doing it at home for nothing."

Young people are in hot demand in North America's sex industry — among pornographers, escort services, massage parlors, and strip clubs. Sex procurers spot kids, recruit them, then supply these outlets first — and as a last resort market the girls directly on the street.

But adolescents and children are usually kept in hotel rooms — out of view of police. Or they are given electronic pagers so they can be called for a paying "date." No matter the outlet, the demand in North America is for younger and younger girls and boys.

"I have guys all the time asking me if I can find them somebody younger," says Tina. Leslie nods her head in agreement.

John Turvey runs Vancouver's Downtown Eastside Youth Activities Society, one of only a few groups in the city working with children caught in prostitution. He says Canadians and Americans should quit wagging fingers at Asia and instead take a hard look at the fast-growing business of renting children for sex in their own North American backyard.

Vancouver, for instance, is a strikingly beautiful city. But it has also gained an ugly reputation — along with Honolulu, Los Angeles, Toronto, New York, and Washington — as a city where it is easy to find a child for sex. In this city of 1.6 million people, there are about 2,000 women in prostitution, 500 of them 17 years and under, child advocates say.

"Young children are in growing demand among 'johns,' guys who would never consider themselves pedophiles," Mr. Turvey says. "They cruise along the 'kiddie strolls' in their minivans with the child-safety seats still attached. . . . Their appetite for kids has created this market."

Vancouver began responding to the problem in late 1994 with a $1.5 million plan to open safe houses and outreach programs. More money flowed in March after an embarrassing report by Turvey's organization that cited little progress, which appeared just prior to the provincial election. But since then few funds have trickled down, workers say.

But if Vancouver has not yet fully come to grips with its problem, neither have American cities, places with squeaky-clean reputations like Wichita, Kansas, Oklahoma City, or Minneapolis, says Frank Barnaba, director of the Paul & Lisa Program, an organization that tries to rescue children from prostitution in New York City.

"What's happening in America is so different from the way it used to be," says Mr. Barnaba. "Pimps used to recruit in the city. But they discovered it's much easier to work the burbs. The kids are naive, materialistic, and vulnerable to the pimp's message. It's the strangest thing I've ever seen."

Money is the driving force. Young girls deliver a dollar premium that older women do not. A 14-year-old girl can make $500 or more a night for a pimp. Or he may sell her for $10,000 or more to another pimp. With the increased demand, sex procurers have expanded their hunt for recruits in the suburbs.

In five recent cases, Barnaba says, kids told him they were recruited in suburban areas that included a clothing store in Cleveland, a tattoo parlor in Minnesota, body-piercing salons in Poughkeepsie and Westchester County, New York, and a movie theater on Long Island, New York.

"A lot of the time naive suburban girls come to the city to hang out and have fun, and within six months they're on the streets prostituting—depending on how much time it takes to brainwash them," says Ericka Moses, who counsels teens at PRIDE, a Minneapolis group trying to help girls and women escape prostitution.

Carmen, a former prostitute who works for a group called WHISPER, seeks out young prostitutes on the streets of Minneapolis. On a bright Monday afternoon, she is walking along East Lake Street—which both she and police agree is a dangerous thing to do no matter what the time of day.

Crack rules around here—and the street corners on East Lake on any Saturday night teem with amateur pimps and the girls and women they prostitute.

On this afternoon, however, Carmen is handing out condoms like candy—trying to inhibit the spread of AIDS by promoting "safe sex"—while at the same time trying to earn the trust of the working girls.

She approaches a sleepy-eyed girl, 17 years old, sitting on a brick wall. "Has he been beating you?" she asks the girl. There is a white substance on her cheek. The girl says "no."

"Why don't you stop working for a while and go get something to eat," Carmen says hopefully. "Here, at least have some of these"—handing over more condoms. She plows on, moving resolutely west on East Lake Street.

Along the street, a gentleman who identifies himself only as "Charlie" sits on a bicycle chewing a toothpick. He has lived around here for years and knows youth prostitution is a booming business these days.

"It's worse now because there's so much more [economic] pressure. It starts with the papa and he puts pressure on the mama, and she puts pressure on the kids. Pretty soon one of them decides he's going to do his own thing."

A roofer, Charlie and his wife have four children. His youngest is 13. He and his wife try to educate and warn her.

"There are a lot of young girls who are vulnerable," he says. "A lot of brothers out here are dog [mean]. They can see the vulnerable girls— and they know what to say. They say, 'Hey sugar, how would you like to make some fast money?' And the girl says, 'Sure.' . . . And pretty soon that's it."

"I talk to my baby girl, and my wife talks to her, and I think she understands," Charlie says. "Least I hope so."

BANGKOK—Those working to stop the sexual exploitation of children say they are not primarily in the business of banning physical acts. They are trying to get people to think differently. And they are still struggling to understand a complex phenomenon that has many faces and causes.

Most discussions of why child sexual exploitation exists begin with poverty. The selling of sex is, after all, a way to earn money. But there is growing evidence that economic circumstance is not as much a cause as people once thought. "I think the poverty argument has been overplayed," argues Vitit Muntarbhorn, a Thai law professor and a former UN special rapporteur on the sale of children. "There are many poor societies that don't exploit children. And there are many rich societies that do."

"Of course poverty is a breeding ground for all sorts of nasty stuff, but there is something much more important going on here," agrees Ron O'Grady, a New Zealander who is the international coordinator of the campaign to End Child Prostitution in Asian Tourism (ECPAT). "When you do an analysis of villages in northern Thailand, you have to ask why is it that in one village, all the girls go automatically into the brothels, while in another village the people would die rather than see their daughters and sons sold off?"

International comparisons are equally intriguing. Thailand is notorious as a destination for sex tourists seeking children. Just to the south is Malaysia, a country of similar economic standing, where child prostitutes are hard to find. "No foreigners would go to Malaysia . . . for sex," Mr. O'Grady adds. "They are similar societies but they have developed in different ways."

So what is the "something much more important" that O'Grady mentions? Phyllis Yanney Abena, a 17-year-old Ghanaian who participated in

Getting Adults to Think in New Ways

Cameron W. Barr

Staff Writer
The Christian Science Monitor

a global conference on the child sex trade held in Stockholm in August, offers this: "The willingness to abuse children all comes down to attitude."

Stemming child sexual exploitation, advocates say, will require that people in many societies reexamine some fundamental ways of thinking: how adults view children, how men think about sex, and how governments respond to an often-ignored aspect of human relations.

Kids Are People, Too

One thing common to most children who are coerced or lured into prostitution is a disrupted home. Of the roughly two-dozen sexually exploited children interviewed for this series, all but one or two had parents who were deceased, divorced, or abusive. Many of them had fled their families for life on the street before being drawn into the sex trade.

This evidence alone suggests that stopping child prostitution begins at home. But advocates argue that society owes children more than parental love and care—it owes them the recognition that they have human rights.

"The problem is not evil individuals," says Moira Rayner, an Australian lawyer who is an expert on child abuse, "but our perception that children are not fully people. We don't believe their stories and we don't teach them their rights," particularly in regard to their bodies.

The United Nations Convention on the Rights of the Child, adopted by the world organization in 1989 and ratified by 187 countries, has gone some way toward promoting the idea that every child has a right to live a life free of sexual exploitation and other abuses. But many people are uncomfortable with these ideas, particularly in societies where filial piety is valued or where offspring are considered parents' property.

Lauran Dale Bethell, an American missionary in Chiang Mai, Thailand, who has spent 10 years running a program designed to keep children out of prostitution, notes that the young women she encounters must contend with powerful feelings of obligation toward their parents. "It's not easy for people to comprehend—that these girls would sacrifice themselves for their families." In Thailand and many other developing countries, children are the only form of social security, so parents nurture a strong sense of duty out of self-preservation.

Talk of children's rights understandably makes some adults anxious. As ECPAT's O'Grady notes, "Once you affirm that children have rights, you cease to have control over them. . . . That's a big shift in our understanding of human values. It means we are no longer thinking we own our children."

Even those charged with law enforcement realize they are not at the core of the battle against the sexual exploitation of children. "In the end we need for all citizens to change their view of what is acceptable behavior," says Laurie Robinson, a US assistant attorney general with the Justice Department.

Men and Sex

With few exceptions, the adults involved in the sexual exploitation of children are men. The women who do participate generally do so on the business side: mothers who sell their daughters into the sex trade or those who act as agents and traffickers. For this reason Mr. Vitit, the Thai law professor, calls for a deeper examination of "irresponsible male sexual behavior."

Various male attitudes toward sexuality contribute to the commercial sexual exploitation of children:

▨ Among Thais, male promiscuity is highly valued. Men at all levels of society may take "minor" wives or maintain mistresses, and some women encourage their husbands to visit prostitutes instead of taking another wife. "It's a tradition here that men buy sex," says Saisuree Chutikul, a one-time member of Thailand's Cabinet and now a government adviser on women's and children's issues. As any visit to a Bangkok brothel will demonstrate, such places are important social centers. These attitudes fuel a sex industry that draws in tens of thousands of people under 18 each year, even according to government statistics. Private groups say the number of child prostitutes in Thailand reaches into the hundreds of thousands.

▨ Many Chinese men prize sexual encounters with virgins, acts that are thought to bring good fortune, rejuvenate aging men, and cure sexually transmitted diseases. Brothel proprietors interviewed in Thailand and Cambodia, countries frequented by sex tourists of Chinese heritage, said they could arrange sex with a virgin for about $450.

⊠ In this age of AIDS, men of many nationalities have sought out virgins and young sexual partners because they are thought to be free of HIV. Analysts of the world's sex industries say this manifestation of the fear of AIDS has increased demand for young prostitutes.

⊠ Research into sex tourism shows that the Western men involved are sometimes driven by an attitude that links sexuality with their sense of identity. O'Grady summarizes: "A lot of men have gotten hurt in Western society by being unable to cope with strong women or with the change in values and have sought new situations in which they could regain their macho-ness. . . ." Sociologists say this desire drives men to seek young, submissive partners—in many cases children.

⊠ Some Japanese are becoming alarmed by a trend that calls into question the sexual attitudes both of middle-aged men and young women. Junior high and high school girls are increasingly prostituting themselves to married men as a way of earning money.

The only thing forcing the girls to sell themselves, according to Eri Aida, a freelance journalist who has spoken to dozens of young women involved in the practice, is peer pressure. They want the same high-priced consumer goods—such as a $500 Prada handbag—that other girls have. The men, Ms. Aida says, either "want to be babied" or seek a submissive partner.

Professor Vitit acknowledges that changing these attitudes will take more than a good publicity campaign. "We have to go back to Square 1," he says, in order to address upbringing, family environment, sex education, and the role of the male in society. "In many of the societies where children are exploited," he adds, "it's a very paradoxical situation where on the one hand there is a taboo in talking about sex and male sexuality. On the other hand, in practice, it's a fait accompli that male sexual behavior is much more free than that of the female, even though that freedom of sexual behavior at times encroaches on other people's rights, including children's rights."

Pedophilia, a condition in which adults have a sexual desire for children, is also a kind of attitude. Activists and experts say that societies must do more to provide treatment for pedophiles, rather than vilifying them as unrepentant child molesters.

"When you see them operating full-scale, and what they do to kids, it's hard to have sympathy," says the Reverend Shay Cullen, an Irish priest based in the Philippines who has been responsible for the arrests of several alleged pedophiles. "But we do have to look back and understand that they, too . . . were often helpless victims [of sexual abuse as children]. . . . It's a very vicious circle."

A Matter of Priorities

In its six years of existence, the ECPAT campaign has done much to raise public awareness about the sexual exploitation of children. The group has targeted an issue that used to be seen as only one of a series of problems affecting children, alongside abuse at the workplace, on the battlefield, and in the home.

One of the group's biggest successes has been to encourage a dozen governments to institute laws barring citizens from sexually exploiting children abroad. Trial courts in Australia and Sweden have convicted citizens for violations of these extraterritorial laws.

Nonetheless, a common complaint from child advocates is that most public officials do not yet take the issue of child sexual exploitation seriously. Police, politicians, and other officials are sometimes involved in the child sex trade or are willing to overlook it.

"You have to have political will if you want to reduce or eradicate child prostitution," says Lina Laigo, the top civil servant in the Philippine Department of Social Welfare and Development.

"That's why I get frustrated sometimes, because [we] also have to contend with the values of our local officials, whether they play politics or whether they have to compromise with their friends or whatever it is. But the thing is we cannot [have them] do what we want them to do because of their other, shall we say, priorities," Ms. Laigo says.

Looking the other way, however, is not limited to public officials. In Nigeria, where older men sometimes take child brides, many people refuse to see the practice as a form of abuse, says Ammuna Alli, of that country's ministry of women's affairs and social development.

"They are not even willing to accept the reality, to admit the existence of the problem," she says.

Father Cullen argues that too many people inhabit what he calls a moral cocoon. "They're not even addressing the issue—that this is an existing, real, moral evil. So constantly we have to point out to them what's actually being done to these children."

Helpful Books and Videos

For Children

These children's books and videos are a sampling of materials designed to help a child deal with such situations as meeting strangers and sexual abuse. Parents should review them before sharing them with children.

The Berenstain Bears Learn About Strangers, by Stan and Jan Berenstain, Random House, New York, NY, 1985, 31 pp. $3.25. An illustrated book for young readers that tells a story about ways children can handle encounters with strangers.

When I Was Little Like You, by Jane Porett, Child Welfare League of America, Washington, DC, 1993, 30 pp. $14.95. An illustrated true story of how a little girl was molested (it is the author's story). A simple, nonsensational, nonfrightening message for a young child, at least as much as possible, considering the subject. Includes ideas on what is proper behavior for adults and what a child can do to prevent and/or stop improper advances of an adult. Briefly mentions counseling of offenders as part of their rehabilitation.

It's OK to Say No!—A Parent-Child Manual for the Protection of Children, by Robin Lenett with Bob Crane, Tom Doherty & Associates, New York, NY, 128 pp. $5.50. The first 30 pages are for parents and include practical advice on how children should deal with strangers. The rest contains short stories that illustrate hypothetical situations.

Winnie the Pooh: Too Smart for Strangers, Walt Disney Home Video, Burbank, CA, 1985, 40 minutes. $29.99. A video on how kids up to middle-school age can be wise regarding strangers. It covers many situations—being home alone, phone calls from strangers, and even sexual abuse. It drives home the message that even though there are "good" strangers out there, by and large, be careful whom you trust.

For Adults and Teenagers

The Safe Child Book: A Common Sense Approach to Protecting Children and Teaching Children to Protect Themselves, by Sherryll Kraizer, Dell Publishing Co., 1985, 127 pp. $11. Mostly for parents, the book includes tips on how to educate kids to protect themselves and also describes warning signs that would indicate that a child is being abused or having other difficulties. Parents are encouraged to keep in touch with their children, and thus avoid what sends kids naively to exploiters.

Safe, Strong, and Streetwise, by Helen Benedict, Little, Brown & Co., Boston, MA, 1987, 176 pp. $5. Much like the above, yet a bit more detailed on various forms of abuse. Includes self-defense techniques. Useful appendix in the back includes references to other groups and publications.

Everything You Need to Know About Sexual Abuse, by Evan Stark, The Rozen Publishing Group, 1993, 63 pp. $15.95. Mostly for a parent to use because of graphic discussion of sexual abuse and the different forms thereof (not only incest).

Runaways, by Keith Elliot Greenberg, Lerner Publishing Co., Minneapolis, MN, 1995, 40 pp. $18.95. Thoughtful account of two young women on why they ran away from oppressive homes and how they escaped from the sex trade.

Where the Lies Take You, Video, 1995, WHISPER (Women Harmed in Systems of Prostitution Engaged in Revolt), Minneapolis, MN. $100 for video/$3 for shipping. It is designed to inform and shock adolescents with stories of former juvenile prostitutes. Language and images are sometimes explicit. Actresses are used to narrate the stories.

Female Juvenile Prostitution: Problems and Responses, National Center for Missing and Exploited Children, Arlington, VA, 1992, 87 pp. Free. A handbook for activists on the topic.

Who's Taking Action

In preparing this series, *Monitor* reporters came across several organizations working to stop the sexual exploitation of children. This list is not exhaustive, nor is it an endorsement.

International

End Child Prostitution in Asian Tourism
328 Phayathai Road
Bangkok 10400 Thailand
Tel: 66-2-215-388
Fax: 66-2-215-8272

US Committee for UNICEF
333 East 38th Street
New York, NY 10016 USA
Tel: 1-800-FOR KIDS
Fax: 212-779-1679

Australia

Come In Youth Resource Centre
457–459 Oxford Street
P.O. Box 39
Paddington, NSW 2021
Tel: 61-2-9331-2691
Fax: 61-2-9331-1583

Brazil

CEDECA
Praia da Conceicão 32
Cidade Baixa
Salvodor, Bahia
Tel: 55-71-2438499

Cambodia

Krousar Thmey
4, Rue 261, Tuk Laak
Tuol Kauk Phnom Penh
Tel: 855-23-366-184
Fax: 855-23-428-946

Cambodian Women's Development Association
P.O. Box 2334
Phnom Penh III
Tel/fax: 855-23-364-050

Canada

Street Teams
P.O. Box 187
Station J
Calgary, Alberta T2A 4X5
Tel: 403-228-3390

Eastern Europe

In the former Communist nations of Europe, private or public agencies helping children in the sex trade are rare or, if they exist, often unstable. In Russia, shelters for street children are a new phenomenon. Many groups, such as Children's Refuge in Lyubertsy, receive aid from European or American sources, such as embassies or religious groups.

Philippines

PREDA Foundation
Upper Kalaklan
Olongapo City 2200
Tel: 63-47-222-4994
Fax: 63-47-222-5573

Thailand

The Foundation for Children/CPCR
666 Charoen-Nakorn Road
Klong Sarn, Bangkok 10600
Tel: 66-2-412-1196
Fax: 66-2-412-9833

Coalition to Fight Against Child Exploitation
P.O. Box 178
Klong Chan, Bangkok 10240
Tel: 66-2-509-5782
Fax: 66-2-519-2794

Daughters' Education Programme
P.O. Box 10 Mae Sai
Chiang Rai 57130
Tel: 66-53-733-186
Fax: 66-53-642-415

New Life Center
P.O. Box 29
Chiang Mai 50000
Tel/Fax: 66-53-244-569

United States

National Center for Missing and Exploited Children
2101 Wilson Boulevard
Suite 550
Arlington, VA 22201-3052
Tel: 800-843-5678

Children of the Night
14530 Sylvan Street
Van Nuys, CA 91411
Tel: 818-908-4474 or
      800-551-1300

Paul & Lisa Program
P.O. Box 348
Westbrook, CT 06498
Tel: 203-767-7660

STOP (Speak Truths On Prostitution)
c/o Grassroots Ministry Alliance
1901 Portland Avenue South
Minneapolis, MN 55404
Tel: 612-872-0684

WHISPER (Women Harmed in Systems of Prostitution Engaged
        in Revolt)
3060 Bloomington Avenue South
Minneapolis, MN 55407
Tel: 612-724-6927

PRIDE (from Prostitution to Independence, Dignity, and Equality)
3125 East Lake Street
Minneapolis, MN 55406
Tel: 612-728-2062

You Didn't Deserve to Be Hurt

Written for
Christian Science Sentinel

THE first sign of child abuse is when you remember how badly you were punished, but can't remember what you did to deserve it. The worst part of my being hit for no reason was that I no longer felt my parents were people who would help me if I got into trouble. When I was in third grade, an older kid undressed me in the park over and over again and touched my private parts, but I never told my parents because I was afraid I'd get hit for that, too.

Families are where you're supposed to learn about love, but sometimes you learn about fear instead. Everyone needs love, lots of it, and if you don't get it at home, you start looking for it in other places. My own hunger to be loved made me look to guys for attention, and eventually sexual involvement led to an unwanted pregnancy. When I finally told my parents, they sent me to a place for unwed mothers.

When bad things happen to you as a child, it makes you feel very dirty inside. I went to Sunday School all my life and I had a lot of nice teachers. It's strange to me now that I never confided in them, but basically I thought secretly I was a very bad person who never could be helped.

The thing I did get from my parents and Sunday School teachers was an introduction to the Bible. My journey into self-worth began when I started reading the Bible on my own in that home for unwed mothers. It was a place sponsored by a Protestant church, and I was really impressed with the people who worked there. It was amazing to me how good they were at loving everybody. Even the girls who were mean and cruel when they first got there became gentle and loving by the time they left. I wanted to learn to love like that. I wanted to be loved like that, especially after the baby was born and put up for adoption. I didn't know it at the time, but that was a prayer to God—asking Him to help me love and be loved.

The turning point came in college when I dated a Christian Scientist who respected the love of God I had found in the Bible. We committed ourselves to a standard of sexual morality, and I could see how it freed both of us to share more of our thoughts and less of our bodies. His self-effacing good humor showed me that I didn't have to take myself so seriously all the time. It was amazing to me to see how his family related to each other—lots of laughter, honesty, and a trust that the children could and would act responsibly. Through the example of this family I found the willingness to work on my relationship with my parents, and a strong, supportive friendship started to develop.

The more I saw and felt how Christian Science was to be lived, the more I wanted to understand how to heal. This led me to take a course in Christian healing, called Primary class instruction, given by an authorized teacher of Christian Science. The class was difficult for me emotionally and mentally, but I treasured learning to define myself in terms of my relation to God as His child. This new understanding of God made me want to dedicate my life to understanding more of how He made me. This was just the opposite of thinking of myself in terms of relationships with others.

When you understand God more deeply, you learn something good about yourself. Because God is Life, we have activity with a purpose and are not stuck in old ways of thinking and acting. God as Soul makes us uniquely individual with talents that deserve to be developed and used in behalf of others. God's love gives us good companionship, which is supportive and not destructive. Spirit tells us that we are not stuck in a material body but can move into broader, more unselfish ways of thinking. God, Mind, gives us good ideas and the wisdom to apply them in our lives. Principle is the name for God that helps us feel safe and secure, even when we can't figure out what's going on. Truth keeps us honest with ourselves and others so we don't start living fantasies or lies.

When my boyfriend started dating someone else a bit later, I wasn't devastated. My identity as God's child was clear enough to me that I knew I could go forward. I started praying for my friends, and some wonderful healings occurred. Even though I never told people much about my past, I could see how the Bible had saved me and could rescue others. As I prayed through their struggles with them, it gave me courage and hope that I could be free of the scars of my childhood and teenage years. The man I married had a pure vision for my healing practice of Christian Science.

The breakthrough in healing my past came through prayer after I was overcome with gratitude for the beauty that had been in my life even when I was an abused child. I found myself thinking about the time when I won first place in a swimming competition. Suddenly I realized that the year I had become a strong swimmer was during the time I was being beaten with a belt. It was very sobering to me, and confusing that there would be two such contradictory things going on. But then I heard a gentle, tender message from God: "No matter how bad things were, it couldn't stop you from going forward." I can't explain in words the feeling of peace that came over me. It was as if a big black cloud had been dissolved and the light was shining right where that bad memory had been. I felt a wholehearted forgiveness for my dad, and gratitude for all the good things he had given me.

The healing of the memory of sexual abuse came almost a decade later. I woke in the morning with another beautiful memory from my childhood. I remembered warm summer days, lying on the grass and gazing up into the fluffy clouds, pretending with my friends that we could see shapes of castles, horses, trees, and everything that delighted us. It was a pure and perfect activity full of the simple pleasure of childhood. I started to cry tears of joy when I heard a voice within saying, "You have never lost your innocence."

That's what I realize has been the basis of my freedom from the past—that I can see my life in terms of the history of innocence and its power, instead of a history of cruelty and disappointment. I wondered at first why the good memories (of the swimming and the summer's day cloud-watching) were so important in displacing the evil things that happened near those times. I have concluded that it is God's way of telling me He really was in my life even though it seemed hard for so many years to see Him. The conviction I have now, and try to share with my friends and people who come for healing, is that every day God is making His love known to us. When I recognize that goodness and appreciate its source in God, the evil doesn't seem so big anymore. As Christ Jesus put it, "Sufficient unto the day is the evil thereof" (Matt. 6:34). To me that means that no matter how much evil seems to be in any one day, it can never outweigh the reality of good.

As I'm writing this I'm thinking of all the other people in the world who might have suffered much worse things than I have. Maybe you are one of them. What seems important to say is: No matter how many times you were hit, raped, burned, or cut, the important thing to remember is that you didn't deserve it. Even if you made a mistake, nobody has the right to hurt you as a way of helping you learn to obey him or her. Nobody has the right to manipulate your body for his or her own pleasure or your pain.

The main reason we can stop feeling and acting like victims is that God has made us a blessing. No matter how many things may have tried to cover up our talents, no matter how few people have been around to support us, nothing can stop the power of God working in us. Man as God's child can't stop doing what he was designed to do—to show others the goodness of God's universe. Man lives good as naturally as a bird sings, the sun rises, the ice yields to the warmth of spring.

The woman who discovered Christian Science, Mary Baker Eddy, didn't suffer physical abuse from other people, but for many years she was sickly, her child was taken from her, she was ridiculed for her work, left poverty-stricken and frequently in need of a home. Her life was restored in a way that made her one of the most generous benefactors of her century. She wrote her primary work, *Science and Health with Key to the Scriptures*. An essential key to her success was her willingness to love her enemies. She prayed often for their freedom and that they would find "the nobler purposes and wider aims of a life made honest: . . . a life wherein calm, self-respected thoughts abide in tabernacles of their own. . . . The sublime summary of an honest life satisfies the mind craving a higher good, and bathes it in the cool waters of peace on earth; till it grows into the full stature of wisdom, reckoning its own by the amount of happiness it has bestowed upon others" (*Miscellaneous Writings*, p. 227).

That's a good description of the freedom we each can expect. God insists that we know who we are as His image. He is communicating that truth every day of our lives, and nothing can stop it from being known to us and to others. Because we are made in a way that is worthy of God's love, none of us deserves to be hurt.

Innocence in the City

Heather M. Hayward

Contributor
Christian Science Sentinel

When 11-year-old Elizabeth and her family moved to a major city, the journey to her new school involved a long subway ride. Her mother commuted with her morning and evening for the first three weeks, to familiarize them both with all the routes she could take. The rush-hour trains were crowded, so it was reasonable to assume that she was well protected. They practiced steps she could take if danger arose.

One day Elizabeth became aware that a man sitting diagonally opposite to her in the crowded subway train was trying to frighten, intimidate, and embarrass her. His covert movements were unseen by the other passengers, but his mocking grin, focused on her, alerted her to moral and physical danger. She was in turn surprised, shocked, and then indignant at his disgusting behavior.

She quickly changed to another train across the platform. He followed, but fortunately the doors closed before he could get inside. He rushed back to the first train and at the next stop tried to intimidate her further by leering at her when the two trains were momentarily parallel. When her mother met her at her home station, she calmly requested that her mother take her to the police so she could report the incident.

From her Christian Science Sunday School education, Elizabeth had become accustomed to turning to God, her heavenly Father-Mother, in prayer. After the encounter in the subway she prayed, with her mother, to see that evil had no power to hurt or harm her, or to fill her thought with nasty pictures and memories. They held to the truth of man as God's pure spiritual idea. They also affirmed that her God-ordained innocence and purity were permanent and inviolate. They rejected any thoughts that there could be a sick-minded individual in God's kingdom trying to corrupt or intimidate. They recalled the words of Christ Jesus "The kingdom of God is within you" (Luke 17:21). They also turned to this statement in Science and Health: "Jesus beheld in Science the perfect man, who appeared to him where sinning mortal man appears to mortals. In this perfect man the Saviour saw God's own likeness, and this correct view of man healed the sick" (pp. 476–477).

Daily, the family dealt with new and diverse challenges that their changed environment brought to their door. They prayed consistently for each individual family member's safety. The whole family was enormously protected from harm through reliance on God. They became more spiritually aware and saw that greater flexibility made each day progressively easier. They adapted to their new situation, moving happily and freely in the community, knowing the absolute control of divine Love.

Even in the busiest streets of a city, we can be comforted by the knowledge that Christ, Truth, is actively present. The holy presence of the all-powerful and all-wise God ensures that every citizen is safe. Our security does not depend on being streetwise, in the usual sense of the word, but on being conscious of the divine presence everywhere, being expressed by everyone.

Although she had one further incident of a similar nature, Elizabeth continued to travel across the metropolis. Her integrity and purity remained untouched, a precious armor against the clamors of sin and sensuality. Her strength, courage, and good humor enabled her to recognize that she could not be haunted by the incident on the subway. The spiritual atmosphere in which she abode, the atmosphere of Spirit, Soul, was the one she truly accepted as her own.

Television pictures of young teenagers being trapped into crime and vice after they run away from home to big cities remind us just how much prayer and God-inspired action are needed. In her first address to The First Church of Christ, Scientist, in 1895, Mary Baker Eddy said: "Beloved children, the world has need of you,—and more as children than as men and women: it needs your innocence, unselfishness, faithful affection, uncontaminated lives. You need also to watch, and pray that you preserve these virtues unstained, and lose them not through contact with the world. What grander ambition is there than to maintain in yourselves what Jesus loved, and to know that your example, more than words, makes morals for mankind!" (*Miscellaneous Writings*, p. 110)

Although the events took place against a backdrop of great challenge, Elizabeth grew to understand more of her right to freedom and peace of mind. She came to recognize her and everyone's absolute invulnerability as the perfect, innocent child of God. Wherever you go, like Elizabeth, there is safety and security for you in the care of divine intelligence and love.

Chapter 7

Resisting

Drugs, Alcohol, and Peer Pressure

Santa Barbara Aims to Knock Out Drug Abuse by "Fighting Back"

David
Holmstrom

Staff Writer
The Christian Science Monitor

SANTA BARBARA, CA—Room H-17—basically ugly. But several old couches are strewn around. A few tables and chairs. Movie posters on the wall. Rock music rumbling. A hole in the wall where the clock used to be.

All conversations in this "drop-in center" at Dos Pueblos High School eventually get around to Scott Guttentag. If you respect and like Mr. Guttentag—and all the "at-risk" teens drifting in and out of H-17 do—you like Fighting Back.

Guttentag is one of nine Youth Service Specialists hired by Fighting Back, Santa Barbara's unique community collaboration. The objective is to confront and reduce—among youths and adults—rampant drug and alcohol abuse in this sunny, affluent, California town.

The lanky teen walking into H-17 to greet Guttentag is Sam Foster, a senior at Dos Pueblos. Santa Barbara was no playground to him. Twisted by a drug overdose not too long ago, he was taken forcibly to a local hospital. "I'd hit bottom," he says. "No place to go or sleep. In the hospital I assaulted a police officer and was chained and beaten by the police. When I woke up, my dad was sitting there with me, and I didn't think he was real. Finally, it all came together and I said, 'What have I done?'"

What Sam and 54 other teens moving in and out of H-17 get from Guttentag is a high-energy advocate who cajoles, pushes, and befriends them away from drugs and alcohol. His litany, offered with humor and trust: Be responsible, study, think about what you are doing.

"Without Scott I would have dropped out of school," Sam says. "I used to have a 1.2 grade average, and now I have a 3.0. I can tell you that Scott has changed a lot of lives around here."

Guttentag delivers a straight message: "Until you experience the consequences of your choices, you won't change your behavior because you don't believe there is a problem."

Fighting Back started six years ago when substance abuse in metropolitan Santa Barbara—population 180,000—had reached proportions close to a public-health crisis. "In the city of Santa Barbara alone," says Chief of Police Richard Breza, "nearly 15 percent of the population was being arrested because of alcohol or drugs."

A 1991 state report concluded that ninth- and eleventh-graders in Santa Barbara were using alcohol and cocaine at a weekly rate 30 percent higher than the state average. And a local hospital said 82 percent of emergency room admissions after 10 PM, including youths, were related to abuse of alcohol and other drugs.

About this time, the Santa Barbara Council on Alcoholism and Drug Abuse hired Penny Jenkins to be director. Mrs. Jenkins, who had lost a daughter to alcohol and suicide, knew that the Robert Wood Johnson Foundation in Princeton, New Jersey, was looking to award $3 million grants to communities ready to combat drugs and alcohol.

If Santa Barbara could design a community-wide plan to attack the problem, a grant might be available. "We were advised to go to the people here who had the greatest influence over the community," she says of her effort to form a board of directors.

Jenkins did this by persuading a who's who of Santa Barbara to give time and resources to a community initiative. In the past, social agencies and institutions tended to operate independently. Now was the time to bring a fresh, collaborative approach to a corrosive problem. New links and programs were needed.

"Until the Fighting Back committee formed, most of us recognized the drug problem here, but we didn't have a sense of ownership about it," says Peter MacDougall, president of Santa Barbara City College and chairman of the Fighting Back Steering Committee. "We thought the courts were taking care of it, or the police. We now know the severe negative effects it has on individuals and a community."

After nearly two years of planning, Santa Barbara was awarded a grant, along with 13 other cities. Now, three years into implementation, Fighting Back initiatives touch almost all corners of the community— in hospitals, courts, jails, schools and businesses. Youth programs, from interns to antigang efforts, are emphasized as the most cost-effective way to divert young people from drug and alcohol abuse. Further funding from the Robert Wood Johnson Foundation is pending.

Many of Fighting Back's nearly two dozen initiatives have changed how the city responds to the following problems:

- At Cottage Hospital, what used to be a Fighting Back early-response team for chemically dependent patients, has become a comprehensive, institutionalized health-care approach.
- A Substance Abuse Treatment Court operates now with a "holistic" approach. After an individual is arrested for a drug-related offense, a court-sanctioned intake team can recommend a treatment program for the judge to approve. Santa Barbara's drug court is one of only five nationwide.
- A gang suppression program in conjunction with the police and district attorney provides a coordinated curriculum in elementary schools for high-risk youth, including parent training.
- A mentoring program at the elementary school level now involves 60 volunteers.
- A summer conference hosted nearly 100 teens in a setting where they created a multicultural society with values, flags, and an Olympics.
- Youth specialists, like Guttentag, also train students in peer mediation and stress management. "The specialists are really successful," says J. R. Richards, the principal of Santa Barbara High School. "If we [should] lose them, then I think we would realize just how effective they have been."

That became apparent in the early stages of Fighting Back, when a few schools balked, denying abuse problems were critical. "Our goal was to get things started . . . not to run the programs," says Jenkins. "The schools are very supportive and pay a portion of youth-worker salaries."

"Scott is a master at talking with kids," says Mike Couch, principal of Dos Pueblos. "I've never seen it before, but kids actually refer themselves to Fighting Back."

Guttentag teaches the alcohol and drug diversion classes for teens suspended from regular school, checks on truancy, and runs the school leadership classes. Of the 66 troubled youths in his charge over the past several years, only two have been resuspended.

"Scott has given me a sense of responsibility," says Denise McFarland, a senior. "Before I didn't care, but he has made me realize I have to graduate if I'm going to get anywhere."

"I've learned a lot," says John Antonio, also a senior. "You come here and you know you have to stop messing around."

Guttentag, who has a degree in psychology, points out that more than 90 percent of the kids who come to the diversion classes are the children of alcoholics and drug addicts. "That makes them different," he says. "It can cause them to be learning disabled. We try to match them with the best teachers and classes, the ones they want, so their chances of succeeding increase.

"Some of the parents have basically handed their kids over to the school. It explains why the kids are struggling. The more parents are involved, the more the kid succeeds."

While Guttentag and other youth specialists nurture teens on a one-to-one basis, another Fighting Back activity is the most popular social event of the year, attracting 8,000 youths.

"I'm Free for the Weekend," held annually, begins with students pledging to stay alcohol- and drug-free for three days. A small purple wristband entitles a student to a host of free and discounted services and entertainment.

This year some 150 Santa Barbara businesses chipped in. Bus rides were free. So was the zoo. The objective? To show that weekends are okay without drugs and alcohol. Try it all week. The program has been so successful that Fighting Back hopes to offer the weekend more frequently. "It gives an excuse to those who don't really want to use drugs, but are pressured into doing drugs," says Alam Jahangiri, a student leader from San Marcos High School. "Now they can say no, not this weekend. People see the weekend as a positive thing. 'I'm Free for The Weekend' says don't do drugs, and they don't. It's a moral thing. They know they have to live with the fact that they signed the pledge."

At San Marcos High School, youth specialist Jennifer Chew oversees many efforts to reach teens, including Friday Night Live, a popular on-campus club started by Ms. Chew that plans drug- and alcohol-free activities and provides safe rides to teens who may have been drinking. This year it was voted club of the year.

"Drugs are everywhere in their lives," says Chew, "and perception is that everybody does drugs. That is a hard thing for them to get past. Some say, 'Everybody I know drinks,' and it is very hard not to fall into that. People don't give teens enough credit. I have high expectations for them. Even the kids from good families with money come in here crying. We have all these programs for at-risk kids, and the truth is that every teen is at risk these days."

Although it is difficult to connect improved county statistical data solely to Fighting Back efforts, there has been a drop in alcohol and cocaine use since 1991. Then the two drugs were being used at a rate 30 percent higher than the state average, and marijuana use was four times the state average. Now, five years later, a Santa Barbara County study concludes that alcohol and cocaine consumption are a little below the state average, and marijuana use is equal to the state average.

Not all community groups have linked with Fighting Back. Because a majority of children in elementary schools are Latino, Latino leaders in Santa Barbara wanted Fighting Back to launch programs at that level.

"A lot of Latino leaders in the community have washed their hands of Fighting Back because of this," says Frank Banales, executive director of Zona Seca, an alcohol and drug treatment program. "Elementary schools should be the target, but I still think Fighting Back is doing good work because the problems are so big."

Jenkins wants more Fighting Back presence in elementary schools: "The intent of the foundation grant was that as the money ran out, the community would start paying for the programs themselves. For some programs that has happened, and others it hasn't."

After 25 years in Santa Barbara, Chief of Police Richard Breza says, "Fighting Back has pulled elements of the community together like I've never seen here before, and we are seeing a down trend in the statistics for drugs and alcohol."

SANTA BARBARA, CA—When it comes to prevention and treatment of substance abuse, the experts agree: What works for Jack in Peoria may not work for Jill in Santa Barbara.

Programs to change behavior are affected by individual family background, age, environment, and the drug being abused. "People want simple answers, and there are none," says Ann Tafe, executive director of the Alcoholism and Drug Abuse Association in Boston. "There are too many levels to treating addiction."

But all treatment and prevention programs go head-to-head with a seductive American irony that contributes to substance abuse and confusion over values for teens. This is the blindspot between the heavy use of alcohol and all kinds of drugs by many adults, and society's desire to keep youths from abusing themselves with substances.

Ask Steve Ainsley, publisher of the *Santa Barbara News Press* about the irony.

When the city council in the nearby town of Carpenteria banned the sale of alcohol on city property for the annual festival, the Chamber of Commerce complained the event would lose money. And a youth-club sponsor said a beer truck at the event was their biggest fund-raiser.

"We wrote an editorial stating that if the festival died because alcohol wasn't served there, then the problem of alcohol is a lot bigger than the festival," Ainsley says. "We got lots of phone calls and letters opposing the editorial. What kind of message are we sending to our kids when Mom and Dad can't go out without drinking?"

Teachers, sociologists, and youth workers across the United States say that most teens not only want guidance from Mom and Dad, but that parents or other adults who offer consistent, low-key advice about drugs and alcohol can make a difference.

It Takes a Community to Fight Drug Abuse

David Holmstrom

Staff Writer
The Christian Science Monitor

"Parents are usually deeply involved in kids' lives in elementary school, and then less so in junior high, and not much in high school," says Mike Couch, principal of Dos Pueblos High School in Santa Barbara. "Frequently, if a student has a problem, the parent or parents have given up, or they don't know what to do."

But the results of several studies refute hopelessness. A study by Big Brothers/Big Sisters of America of nearly 1,000 children from ages 10 to 16 found that children from low-income households with mentors were 46 percent less likely to begin using illegal drugs than other kids, and 27 percent were less likely to begin to use alcohol at all.

A study by The Partnership for a Drug-Free America found that teens who reported learning about the risks of marijuana from their parents were half as likely to smoke it as those who hadn't. But even with parental discussions about marijuana, about 21 percent of the teens in the study went ahead and smoked marijuana.

This illustrates the difficulty of intervening successfully in the lives of many young people. Either from peer pressure, or seeing adults in their families use drugs, or because they believe media glamour, they experiment. And because alcohol and drugs persist within a larger community, many activists now endorse a "holistic" approach to prevention and treatment.

"People are beginning to understand that this notion of coming together as a whole community to deal with these problems means that nobody has the answer by themselves," says Paul Jellinek, vice president of the Robert Wood Johnson Foundation, which funds a number of community projects.

"Successful programs now and in the past," says Kathy Akerlund, a prevention specialist for Colorado's Alcohol and Drug Abuse Prevention Services, "generally have multiple strategies, not short-term programs, but long-term with plenty of options like tutoring, mentoring, getting the family involved."

The community-wide approach puts less of a focus on specific youth problems after they occur, instead paying more attention to strengthening the support of children in crucial developmental stages.

This means viewing families and teens as valued entities in the community. Schools, churches, and health-care and law-enforcement agencies organize in new ways. In turn, the community is strengthened.

In Minnesota, a three-year project confirmed the validity of using a community strategy. Project Northland combined classroom and community interventions to prevent alcohol use by teens in 24 school districts. Some 90 percent of parents also became involved.

By combining skills training in school and alcohol-free extracurricular activities linked to the community, the project reduced the onset of alcohol use by 28 percent.

A Tough Sell: Breaking Away from Gangs

David
Holmstrom

Staff Writer
The Christian Science Monitor

BOSTON—Jack has an easy manner, almost a baby face. It's hard to imagine him with a gun in his hand, aiming at somebody and pulling the trigger. He admits to that, to dealing drugs, too, and more.

At 16 years old, he is incarcerated for carrying a gun. Seated in a small room at the Massachusetts Department of Youth Services (DYS) facility, he wanders a little as he talks. "People join gangs because they think it's their family," he says. "It wasn't like that when I was in a gang. As soon as you get locked up they forget about you. It's all a big game. You play the game and learn the hard way at the end."

Six months ago, Jack welcomed this quick foray into a little self-realization. He had been part of a gang while staying with his grandmother, hoping to get back with his mother in another part of Boston. While inside the facility, he got involved with Teen Empowerment, a group that helps at-risk teens learn how to be leaders.

But like so many streetwise teens who slide back and forth between doing wrong and occasionally thinking right, Jack flopped over again on the wrong side. Not too long after he was released, he broke the conditions of his probation by being out at night. He's back in DYS for at least 30 days.

Experts readily agree that pulling teens out of gangs, or preventing them from joining, may be the most difficult task involved in the array of programs aimed at rescuing youths. The main culprit: the influence of the street.

"Peer pressure is the black hole that sucks kids out of their houses," says Bill Stewart, assistant chief probation officer for Massachusetts District Court in Dorchester, a neighborhood in Boston. "In my opinion, it is the main cause of gangs."

Just at the age when many inner-city and suburban teens need family support, or mentors, or memorable teachers—and answers to the age-old question of "what am I for?"—they are lured by the idea of belonging to a cool, tough "family" where bad is good.

So, for the Jacks of the streets, the cycle continues. Poverty, peer pressure, drugs, alcohol, no parental control, violent movies and rap music—living in a spiritual void, they gather in gangs looking for respect. They war against each other and society in big and small cities all over the country. Kids are lured by the idea of belonging to a cool "family" but find membership offers them little long-term support.

Experts disagree on gang numbers. Malcolm Klein, author of *The American Street Gang*, says there are half a million gang members across the United States. The National Gang Crime Research Center at Chicago State University in Illinois puts the number at 1.5 million. But the most recent Department of Justice report for 1995 estimates the number of gangs in the United States at 23,378, with 664,906 members.

No single definition fits all gangs. Some exist for illicit commercial reasons; others are strictly ethnic, with their origins stretching back for decades. Others claim a neighborhood or "turf" area, and some spread graffiti as wannabes rather than serious gangs. Other gangs form and dissolve in weeks or months.

Once in, most members get caught up in a life of fear and uncertainty. "It's like they are playing poker," Mr. Stewart says, "always raising each other, and they have to [deliver] if they want to keep the image as being the baddest of the bad."

Ex-gang members say that eventually, many hard-core bangers either end up dead, or simply try to escape alive.

"When I joined a gang at 14, it was for protection, and because I wanted to belong to something, anything," says Armando Gonzalez, a counselor for the Gang Prevention Intervention program in Long Beach, California, and a church pastor. "I wanted to feel proud. 'Now I'll get some attention,' I thought."

A Spiritual Helping Hand

After five years of gang-banging, gunfire, fighting, and drugs, he wanted out. "I just got tired of it," he says, "tired of going in and out of jail, and tired of seeing my friends killed. I had become a drug addict, and fighting it was hard." Although he faltered along the way, he eventually turned to God, found compassion for himself and his fellow man, and turned to religion.

For Manuel Ortiz, a former gang leader in Guatemala and later in Phoenix, Arizona, years of violence and drug dealing yielded to a sense that God was getting closer.

"I was in an alley selling marijuana to a guy," he says, "and I heard a voice telling me to stop. I turned around, thinking somebody was there. But nobody was there. The guy says, 'Hey, c'mon, you going to sell me the stuff or not?' I heard the voice again telling me I was doing bad things to people. I wasn't on drugs or drunk. I started to cry, and knew I had to stop dealing."

A month later, he and his associates were caught in a drug bust. "Everybody went to jail but me," he says. "This was my exit that God provided me. I couldn't have just said to them, I'm not selling anymore because they might have killed me. So when they got busted, that was the end for me. I called a friend and said I was ready to learn about God."

While ex-gang members like Mr. Gonzalez and Mr. Ortiz broke from gangs by discovering God, dozens of organizations, schools, and communities in the nation are implementing intervention and prevention programs.

One of the most successful is The Omega Boys Club in San Francisco. Started by two public school teachers, the program offers regular mentoring and peer counseling to at-risk teens, and often recruits teens while they are in the city's juvenile-detention facility.

The unifying theme of the club centers on African-American culture and promotes extended family, viewing elders as teachers, and the values of education and achievement. By joining Omega, teens are helped in their development to be responsible to themselves and the "family" of Omega. They take a pledge not to use drugs or violence, and attend regular "family" meetings.

Currently, more than 64 club members are enrolled in college; 31 have graduated. Many previously were failing in school.

Joe Marshall, a founder of the club, says Omega's three-step process works inside the family concept. "First, we deal with the risk factors that contribute to violent behavior," he says. "Then we eliminate the anger, fear, and pain in the young person, and prescribe new rules for living to replace the code of the streets that they once lived by." Omega also airs "Street Soldiers," a popular nightly talk-radio program that the *New*

Yorker magazine called "a kind of electronic parent for violence-prone young people."

The lives of most gang members are lacking the resources available to teens with solid support from their families. Beverly Deep, superintendent of Westlake City Schools in Westlake, Ohio, interviewed several hundred black male gang members between 1988 and 1993.

"Most kids go through periods when there are voids to be filled," she says. "But for almost all of the teens I interviewed, nothing filled the void. So they chose the gang to be accepted, needed. They may have to kill somebody to get it, but they think they will get it in the gang."

Worsening Gang Problems		
Cities and counties reporting 1995 gang activity	**2,007**	
Number of gangs	**23,378**	
Number of gang members	**664,906**	
Cities and counties reporting no 1995 gang activity	**1,433**	
Report of gang problem by 2,007 of the agencies that reported 1995 gang activity	**Getting better: 10%** **About the same: 41%** **Getting worse: 49%**	
Likelihood of near-term gang problem by agencies that reported no 1995 gang activity	**High likelihood: 7%** **Medium likelihood: 30%** **Low likelihood: 55%** **No likelihood: 8%**	

Source: U.S. Department of Justice

Intervention in a Crisis

Another promising program in Oakland, California, literally intervenes in emergency rooms. Caught in the Crossfire, a program of Teens on Target, counsels teens who are hospitalized for gunshot wounds. "In that crisis moment," says Tamara Milagros of Teens on Target, "our immediate goal is to reduce retaliation. One of our counselors will often meet with the teens who brought the victim and then do follow-up counseling."

Counselors try to diffuse the anger by exploring alternative strategies to violence; helping to develop a plan for staying safe; or setting up an ongoing program to keep victims or others from rejoining gangs.

Since it began two years ago, 120 victims have been counseled. "We're there to intervene at a moment when there is the most potential for those individuals wanting to make a change," Ms. Milagros says.

For Ortiz, who is now attending college in Phoenix and counseling youths about spirituality, conveying the cruel realities of gangs is a challenging task. "Everybody believes the gang is a family," he says. "But it isn't. You go to jail, they don't visit you. You go to the hospital, they don't really care. Yeah, but when you die, everybody shows up at your funeral."

The latest study from the U.S. Department of Justice's Office of Juvenile Justice found growing concerns about worsening gang problems in cities and counties. The study surveyed 4,120 cities' counties. Figures on the extent of gang membership and activity vary widely among studies.

Psychiatrist Jack C. Westman, who has spent decades working with neglected and abused children, is preaching an offbeat message. He'd like to see the licensing of parents, making parenthood a privilege rather than a right. He's quoted as saying: "I have found that the people who do [neglect and abuse their children] are not able to handle responsibility for their own lives, much less the lives of children. So what I'm trying to do is help the public make that appreciation — it really is the quality of parenting that counts."[1]

Actually, parenting is a task where quality and quantity both count. For responsible parenting, you generally have to have a great quantity of being there for the quality of your care to come through. Being there defeats neglect, which itself is a form of abuse. Being there shuts down a whole range of unhappy scenarios for unsupervised children. Being there can send a loud message to kids that they are loved and that they count.

The race against child-rearing disasters stumbles at the start without responsible parents present. Licensing parents is not the key. But responsible parenting is necessary. It can be appreciated. It can be prayed for. It can be learned. That's important, since the moral maturity needed to raise a child is not born of the biological capacity to produce one.

It's natural that parents should want to do the right thing. And they have from God all that they need to succeed. It's inherent in their real being, as God's likeness, to express the limitless capacities of His nature.

Models of good parenting are needed. Some of the best are in the Bible. Consider Christ Jesus' parable of the prodigal. It's been read in many ways: as a story of parental love that never abandons, as a story of misspent time reclaimed, as a story of self-absorption overcome by unselfish love. Have you read it as a story of being there? Remember how the prodigal left

Being There for Your Children

Channing Walker

Contributing Editor
The Christian Science Journal

home and recklessly wasted all he had? The Bible says that when he finally resolved to return home, his father saw him "a great way off."[2] Did the father see him at a distance because the father had never, in a sense, taken his eyes off him, never stopped beholding the son's true selfhood? We might say the father was being there with the son even when he couldn't be physically present with him. Nothing pulled the father off his watch.

"Father-Mother," writes Mary Baker Eddy in *Science and Health*, "is the name for Deity, which indicates His tender relationship to His spiritual creation."[3] Does that surprise you as it did me at first? I'd have guessed Father-Mother would indicate man's origin. But the divine Parent isn't just the creator of man. He is ever present. He has a tender and continuous relationship with each of His children. A so-called human creator can produce, then disappear. With kids that spells neglect. But our Father-Mother never leaves. This fact, realized—and lived through the expression of God's fathering and mothering qualities—is the spiritual underpinning that helps parents be there in positive, ongoing ways for their children.

Parents who abandon children, parents who believe they have no time, parents sunk in self-absorption—all three types of neglect are within the limitless healing reach of Father-Mother God.

It's usually only in the face of huge personal problems that a parent deserts a child. Perhaps serious substance abuse haunts a parent, or parents may literally be children themselves. The backup system of social workers, courts, foster homes, is, in the United States at least, overwhelmed. To take just one need that may therefore go unmet in this system: the presence of good role models. There are many wrong models for kids. One that is always wrong for a child is to have no positive role model at all.

How can we help? We can look hard at what children are confronted with. We can look hard, but also look from on high, so to speak, seeking the God's-eye view. Right where a sad story appears, Christ—God's saving influence—is there to heal and restore. Christ is the spirit of Love, always present to enlighten human consciousness. Christ reveals to consciousness the actual, spiritual nature of man, the wholeness of man, the invulnerability of man, the indestructibility of man. And Christ does this even in that void where no right models are presented to kids. Prayer in which we glimpse that the Christ is present and active, and realize the truth of man, brings the divine power to bear on the human scene. Then solutions become apparent. Correcting, healing actions take place.

Social workers and other decision makers are not outside the influence of prayer. And children, even if they can't explain why, begin to feel the spirit of Love being there for them, filling the void, presenting them with guidance and nurturing. The Christian Science textbook, *Science and Health*, assures us, "Christ presents the indestructible man, whom Spirit creates, constitutes, and governs."[4]

For most parents, not being there doesn't stem from indifference but from the belief that they have no time. This may especially be true for the single parent. Are schedules a jumble of obligations — jobs, appointments, meals? No wonder they overcrowd and time with children evaporates. But dominion over time is possible. It comes less from a willful drive for control and more from a quiet awareness of Spirit governing every event of our days.

Don't be surprised if this calm, spiritual awareness brings to light possibilities before unseen. We might find, like Hagar — a single mother in the Bible — that what's most needed can be found where least expected.[5] Today's parent may not discover a well of water in the desert, but his or her eyes can be opened to find a block of time right where it seemed there was none available.

Spirit is the source and substance of all real being. So, what constitutes our days? Exchange the jumble-of-obligations view for a sense of daily life as the ongoing unfoldment of Spirit's plan for all of Spirit's creation. Unfoldment occurs in consciousness but appears in experience. Water is found in the desert. Time opens up. The spaciousness of Spirit does not crowd. Instead of racing against deadlines, we find our days flowing more smoothly. Obligations at home and work become opportunities for parents to bless and to be blessed. And the business of blessing is never at odds with itself or out of time. Spirit's ongoing and tender relationship with man sustains parents in being there for their kids.

What about parents who are sunk in self-absorption? A sports fan glued to the final minutes of a tense Super Bowl game may seem unreachable even by those with him. If the effort to pull him away is to save him from a burning house, he'll eventually be grateful. The household of a self-absorbed parent is very possibly in a slow burn. Neglect happens. Whether spawned by marital worries, an obsession with food (or a worse addiction), or by financial fears, self-absorption blinds and deafens a parent. A child crumbling right before him goes unnoticed.

The good news: self-absorption can be healed through unselfed love. Even if a parent has become a prodigal—his time spent absorbed in his own concerns, oblivious to family—his obsession and fears have no intrinsic power. For instance, financial woes don't really have the power to suck someone's whole attention in on himself, unless he chooses to give them this power.

We are here to love all God's creation, beginning with our families. When a pure love for others becomes more real to us than what we fear, self-absorption ends. Unselfed love quenches a smoldering scene. A free flow of unselfish acts then follows. A parent's breaking his or her own fixation on television viewing, or money troubles, or whatever, may take repeated effort. But it also brings ongoing blessing. *Science and Health* makes this encouraging statement: "Whatever holds human thought in line with unselfed love, receives directly the divine power."[6]

Father-Mother God holds each of us in perfect, tender relation to Himself. The substance of that relationship is love, love that is more than unselfish, love that expresses the purity of divine Love itself. Divine Love is there for each parent—and for each child—and it is, ultimately, irresistible. Father-Mother God embraces us, and the power of our divine Parent is without limit, fully able to draw someone out of a self-involved, self-absorbed state. Love, deeply felt in prayer, breaks the spell. Then the abuse of neglect doesn't happen—healing does.

Father-Mother God maintains a tender and ongoing relationship with His offspring. This spiritual fact is the underpinning enabling parents to be there for their kids. Parental neglect, whether in the form of abandonment, lack of time, or self-absorption, begins to give way. Then parenting is seen as the privilege it is. A child's right to freedom from neglect comes into focus. And society as a whole is blessed.

---

1 *Los Angeles Times*, February 8, 1995.   2 Luke 15:20.   3 *Science and Health*, p. 332.
4 *Ibid.*, p. 316.   5 See Genesis 21:9–20.   6 *Science and Health*, p. 192.

When our daughter was to be bused to a school in another district, downtown, I inquired about it. Yes, the teaching was done well, but discipline problems were plentiful. One parent who lives in the district was driving her children to another school. "I would be afraid to put my little girl on that playground," she said.

I thought of changing schools, too, but realized that, at this point, such action would have been based on fear, and it wouldn't necessarily provide my daughter with safety. I thought of Christ Jesus. He proved life to be safe in God, Spirit. Hatred and ignorance couldn't touch his life, because he understood it to be spiritual. Jesus' actions were impelled by God, Love, not fear.

So I stopped listening to and rehearsing the stories about this school and instead let divine Love guide my thought. I decided to pursue a spiritual view of education and safety.

The Bible says: "All thy children shall be taught of the Lord; and great shall be the peace of thy children. In righteousness shalt thou be established: thou shalt be far from oppression; for thou shalt not fear: and from terror; for it shall not come near thee" (Isa. 54:13, 14). This idea of God being the Teacher became a rock on which I could stand firm in the conviction that safety is a normal and constant factor in children's lives, whatever school they attend.

The quality of a school reflects the quality of the thoughts being expressed there. Inspiration, respect, tolerance, receptivity, are what people want in schools. However, these attributes must be seen as provided by God. If for a moment we assume that it's certain people—a certain staff and school population—who are the source of good qualities, we are not seeking the surest safety. God is the origin of all true thought and action. What kind of a God do we have?

The Bible relates a God of patience, mercy, and wisdom. These qualities are constantly being reflected

School in Safety

Cheryl F. M. Petersen

Contributor
Christian Science Sentinel

by His creation. God is Mind. This makes sense: one Mind governing the entire creation with understanding and wisdom. One Mind, divine Love, governing every child in my daughter's school. Divine Love influences and stimulates. Love is definitely not limiting. It is always expecting and seeing the best in every individual. This Teacher provides a safe environment for progress.

No more thinking of school environment in terms of material buildings, mortal genders, and mixed races, I decided. Instead, I recognized school to be a place where God is always being expressed through spiritual qualities, such as wisdom, integrity, and obedience. These attributes of God are available impartially and continuously. This passage from *Science and Health with Key to the Scriptures* by Mary Baker Eddy was a light on my path, assuring me that good was the ruling influence in my daughter's school: "Moral and spiritual might belong to Spirit, who holds the 'wind in His fists;' and this teaching accords with Science and harmony. In Science, you can have no power opposed to God, and the physical senses must give up their false testimony" (p. 192).

The sentences that follow that statement gave me a rule for taking action: "Your influence for good depends upon the weight you throw into the right scale. The good you do and embody gives you the only power obtainable. Evil is not power." I practiced doing this. For instance, whether in the grocery store or on our farm, I made sure only respectable conversation was being shared. Others followed my example and it became fun. I lost the fear that some people were incapable of expressing Godlike qualities. God created man as spiritual, able to forgive, uplift, and progress.

Well, school started and our daughter not only went to school with joy but also came home with joy. A regular time for me to help in her first-grade classroom came up naturally. Each time I went to the school, I specifically observed and thanked God for all the evidence of morality—all the expressions of honesty, grace, attentiveness, and responsibility.

Months passed, and a friend employed at this school mentioned her wonder and gratitude that this year "there just are not the discipline problems like last year." She didn't know where they had gone. Now, I know I was not the only one praying or desiring integrity. Good behavior was being valued and nurtured throughout the school.

One day the school sent a notice to all the students' homes, warning of a white van trying to pick up children walking home. I reminded myself that safety is not confined to a place. Everyone's Father-Mother God is everywhere. As I walked to school for my weekly visits, I now diligently denied that ignorance, prejudice, and lack had any place or power where God is. Godlike qualities, such as compassion, meekness, and perceptiveness are always present—and can take form in many ways.

This was proved when, just off the school grounds, a fight broke out between older boys. A truck stopped, and a man jumped out and immediately broke up the fight. He quietly spoke with the boys. No yelling. Just a termination of the discord. Where did that man come from? This example of the keen presence of God's power is still an inspiration to me.

The issue about the white van quickly dissipated. Instead, love for morality more and more appeared.

Another day while I was quietly listening to God, which is how I think of prayer, the idea of calm, poise, and order being ever present came clearly to me. There is no sense of panic in God's creation. When I got home that afternoon, our daughter gave us a note from the principal. It began, "Safety first!" A locked briefcase had been delivered to the office that day. The deliverer had been unfamiliar and the message unclear. The possibility of a bomb threat was handled with perfect poise. In an effort to evacuate the school in an orderly fashion, the fire alarm was set off. The staff and children left the building calmly, thinking it was just a drill. They were taken to another facility until a police investigation found that all was well.

"All thy children shall be taught of the Lord . . . ." No matter what the situation, God is always instructing His children in an intelligent way. Because God is the true Teacher, their moral development is protected from evil influences. Because divine Love is the only source of thought, fear or ignorance cannot penetrate consciousness. Knowing these truths helps to establish safety at school.

As it turned out, the principal of this school was chosen that year as the regional "Principal of the Year." And the parent first mentioned in this article is now sending her daughter to this school. True learning—learning of the ever-presence of goodness—is universal and all-inclusive.

Chapter 8

Defusing
Neighborhood Conflict

Neighborhood Defense: Watchful Eyes, Caring Hearts

Marilyn Gardner

Staff Writer
The Christian Science Monitor

BOSTON—Theodore Lewis, a senior at Glen Oaks High School in Baton Rouge, Louisiana, remembers well the tense atmosphere that often shrouded the school during his freshman year.

"You couldn't have a lot of meetings for the whole school because it would be so crowded, and tempers would flare, and a fight would start," says Theodore, a parliamentarian in the student government. "If teachers didn't break it up, it would just go on until they got tired of fighting."

To avoid such incidents, administrators canceled pep rallies, dances, and talent shows—a solution that satisfied no one. Then Tommy Stout, a parent, came up with a better idea. He recruited a dozen fathers, many of whom work shifts and are home during the day, to be a calming presence in the school, walking the halls, monitoring the cafeteria, and attending major school activities. The program, called Security Dads, is modeled after one that began in Indianapolis five years ago.

"We don't try to take the place of the school security," Mr. Stout explains. "We're just a group of dads who want to get involved and help save our children."

Across the country, that earnest desire to keep children safe and prevent violence is motivating concerned parents and community members to band together in a variety of efforts. Some are as simple as walking children to and from school. Others involve school-based groups such as Security Dads, neighborhood watches, and after-school programs.

Armed with nothing more than caring hearts and compassionate spirits, volunteers find strength in the collective power of many watchful eyes and listening ears. Some also serve as helping hands to traditional authority figures such as school administrators and police officers.

Because groups like these are so varied, no figures exist to measure their numbers. And ironically, the groups are springing up even when threats are minimal. Although statistics indicate that crime is down, "there is a widespread perception of lack of safety" fed by news stories, TV shows, and movies, says Samuel Mark, assistant vice president of civic and community relations at the University of Southern California. "I feel that the perception of violence is much worse than the actual reality," he says.

At Glen Oaks High School, the Security Dads, who now number about 50, have made an impressive difference. Social activities have resumed, and the school "has turned around 110 percent," says Stout, who spends about 20 hours a week there.

"We haven't had any serious problems in two years," adds Stan LeBlanc, principal. "It's been a godsend. They're just a super bunch to have on campus."

For students, many of whom live in single-parent homes, the fathers' presence goes beyond maintaining order. "When you're down and you need somebody to talk to, you can always talk to Security Dads," says Lewis, the student parliamentarian.

And talk they do. "Students can confide in the Dads better than they can in us, even telling them stuff they want us to find out," says LeBlanc.

So successful is the program that it has expanded to three high schools in Baton Rouge and two others in the state.

Creating a safe environment at school represents only one solution, of course. In Los Angeles, neighbors surrounding the University of Southern California's University Park campus have taken another approach—keeping their eyes on children as they walk to and from school. Volunteers in a program called Kid Watch often spend time outdoors from 8 AM to 9 AM and from 3 PM to 4 PM.

"I'm usually outside, working in my garden, reading on the porch, or talking to my neighbors," says Juanita Judice, a volunteer.

Although most of the 63 approved Kid Watch sites are homes, the group is also recruiting businesses, churches, and nonprofit agencies. Children receive an orientation at school, along with a wallet card listing emergency numbers.

Dr. Mark offers one measure of the program's effectiveness: "We hear from the Los Angeles Police Department that they get many fewer calls for problems in streets where we have a lot of Kid Watch volunteers," he says. "People feel Kid Watch is having an effect on driving away crime."

Even before Kid Watch began, Norma Montgomery, the mother of three daughters, maintained vigilance in the neighborhood. "I caught two young guys trying to steal a Raiders jacket from a little boy one time," she says. "I yelled at them, and they ran away."

In another incident three years ago, Mrs. Montgomery stood up to nearly 20 gang members who appeared uninvited at a block party. "I just confronted them and told them they were welcome to join the party, but we would have none of their gang activities," she says. "I asked them their names, and they told me. They sat down, and we served them food. Then they thanked us and left."

The following August, the young men returned, bringing friends with them. "They were just so nice," Montgomery recalls. "You wouldn't know they were the same gang members."

Speaking of her decision to confront the teenagers, she adds, "I know some people would say that's a silly thing to do. But there comes a time in your life when you have to stand up for what you believe is right."

In other cities, the national McGruff House Safety Program offers children similar protection by establishing neighborhood homes as reliable sources of help if they are threatened, hurt, or lost. Participating homes display a sign featuring McGruff the Crime Dog.

Betty Kostelac, a McGruff House volunteer in Kansas City, Missouri, says, "It's just a matter of being a good citizen to everyone."

Mrs. Kostelac, who is retired, sees another long-term advantage. "Those children, as they grow up, are going to realize that they too can help someday by doing this sort of thing," she says.

Such programs are not without challenges. In Kansas City, efforts to recruit McGruff House volunteers have been slower than leaders expected. Roxane Johnson, coordinator of community outreach for the Kansas City school district, finds that some people are reluctant to undergo a police check—a standard requirement in many such programs.

Another city effort has been "McGruff Trucks," or designated utility trucks. "If kids see a utility truck with that logo, they know to go up to that truck if they're in trouble," says Ms. Johnson. "The driver will use a mobile phone to call for help. That gives us thousands more outlets."

After-school programs also play a role in keeping children safe. Some programs, such as those in Trenton, New Jersey, are held in schools. Others are smaller-scale.

Until last year, for example, the 300-home Raineshaven neighborhood in Memphis had many latchkey children simply "hanging out" after school. So Estelle Paulette and Queen Smith created the Raineshaven Youth Council. Meeting in the neighborhood's Golden United Methodist Church, they hold workshops on such topics as gangs and sexual awareness. They also take students on outings.

In the neighborhoods served by Kid Watch in Los Angeles, group outings serve another purpose. "We're trying to get children to use the parks, three wonderful museums in the area, and the library, but sometimes they hesitate because of the fear of something happening to them," says Mark.

Kid Watch staff members give parents and children tours of museums, a sports arena, and the university. They also map out "safe routes" for children to use.

Whatever the community's endeavor, Annette Kessler, principal of the L.B. Weemes Elementary School in Los Angeles, sees the potential for a ripple effect.

"You get this little circle of people feeling good, and they help other people to feel good and safe," she says. "The good feelings people have about their community start to provide security to more and more people. It outweighs the impact of the very few negative people who right now indirectly control the neighborhood by making you stay behind locked doors."

Where to Find More Information

- McGruff House Safety Programs, National Crime Prevention Council, 1700 K Street, NW, Second Floor, Washington, DC 20006-3817. Phone: 202–466–6272.
- Security Dads, Inc. 4419 Barnor Drive, Indianapolis, IN 46226. Phone: 317–549–3553; 317–226–3848.
- "Promising Initiatives for Addressing School Violence," April 1995 (U.S. General Accounting Office, Washington). To order by phone, call: 202-512-6000.
- *Waging Peace in Our Schools*, Linda Lantieri and Janet Patti (Boston: Beacon Press, 1996).

Schools Try Conflict Resolution to Help Students Stay Focused on Facts, Not Fights

Seth G. Jones

Staff Writer
The Christian Science Monitor

New York—On the surface, Primary School 198 here is no different from many other inner-city schools: It is beset by chronic violence that shows few signs of abating. But while many schools are installing more metal detectors or getting tougher with young criminals, P.S. 198 is taking innovative steps to teach students how to counter school violence.

One afternoon late last year, for example, fifth-grader Carlos Quintero was in the school's cafeteria when a fight broke out between two of his friends. Instead of watching the boys exchange punches or waiting for a teacher, he offered to help.

"I took them into the gym," he recalls. "I asked them what happened and then I asked them how they felt." After several minutes of talking, Carlos explains, the two boys calmed down and apologized to each other. "They didn't fight anymore, and they became friends," he says.

Carlos was no ordinary student offering to help. He has been trained as a mediator as part of the curriculum designed by the New York-based Resolving Conflict Creatively Program (RCCP).

Established in 1985 by Educators for Social Responsibility Metropolitan (New York) Area and the New York City Board of Education, RCCP is a school-based program in conflict resolution and intergroup relations. It serves more than 150,000 children in 325 schools from Brooklyn, New York, to Anchorage, Alaska.

Modern-day conflict resolution traces its roots to the 1920s, when educators sought to improve relations between labor groups and management, according to Linda Lantieri, cofounder and national director of RCCP. It enjoyed a renaissance in the 1980s, when numerous books that offered step-by-step tips on how to negotiate conflicts at work and at home hit the bestseller lists.

Today, many schools are turning to it as yet another way to tackle the conflict and violence among youths that has crept into school halls.

According to FBI estimates, for instance, juvenile arrest rates for violent crimes more than tripled between 1965 and 1990. In a study released earlier this year by James Fox, dean of the College of Criminal Justice at Northeastern University in Boston, murders by teens between the ages of 14 and 17 increased 172 percent from 1985 to 1994.

The problem, of course, is not limited to urban areas. "Violence is not just an inner-city problem," says Ms. Lantieri. "Violence is America's problem. And programs like RCCP are not only about stopping the violence. They're about increasing the climate of nonviolence."

Conflict-resolution programs are by no means limited to tough city schools. Indeed, the second school system where RCCP was established is in Anchorage, Alaska. Lantieri estimates that there are thousands of organizations implementing conflict resolution programs in schools and communities throughout the United States.

And there are a variety of approaches. In Detroit, Alicia Reneé Farris runs a conflict resolution organization called the Youth Nonviolence Training Program (YNTP). Created in 1992, it is community-based and springs from the teachings of Martin Luther King, Jr. "Our basic philosophy is to establish a cadre of nonviolent leaders," says Ms. Farris. "And everything is built around the nonviolent social activism of Dr. King."

YNTP has a two-pronged approach. It teaches kids teamwork, how to defuse disagreements, and success-sustaining strategies—and then has them perform community-service projects. It also organizes events such as rap concerts and costume balls that have positive, nonviolent messages.

Unlike YNTP, the RCCP curriculum is more school-oriented and involves an amalgam of lessons built into the school day. Students learn to communicate and cooperate, acknowledge other people's feelings, and appreciate diversity. RCCP staffers also work with parents to foster a peaceful environment at home.

Some experts argue that it's important to start teaching conflict-resolution skills at a young age. "It's better to help build the child than to rebuild the teenager," says Mr. Fox. "And it's considerably less expensive."

Student response at P.S. 198 has been largely positive. "I feel like I'm making a difference. I'm helping people listen to each other," says Ashley Hempstead, a fifth-grader. "We have the opportunity to cause less fights and more peace," says Todd Bradley, another fifth-grader.

Carlos Quintero says that what he learned has reached into his life beyond the schoolyard. "Last spring, I was playing in a baseball game and a kid on the other team wanted to fight," Carlos recalls. "I said no and walked away."

Some experts, however, question the overall efficacy of conflict resolution programs. Jack Levin, director of the Program for the Study of Violence and Conflict at Northeastern University in Boston, who is doing a study of school-based violence prevention and reduction programs throughout Massachusetts, contends that schools should concentrate more on keeping kids busy both before and after school.

"These [conflict-resolution] programs simply are ineffective when it comes to extreme forms of violence—the very forms of violence that seem to be plaguing our major cities now," he says. "If we really want to do something about violence . . . we have to provide healthy alternatives."

He recommends lengthening the school day so that students are supervised while their parents work and offering kids productive alternatives such as summer jobs, after-school athletic programs, and adequate and effective day care.

Others argue that implementing conflict resolution programs in schools will do little good unless schools undergo more fundamental changes.

"It's like rearranging deck chairs on the Titanic," says Terry Moe, senior fellow at the Hoover Institution in Palo Alto, California, and professor of political science at Stanford University. "You can have these programs, but if the underlying problem is more fundamental, the programs aren't going to work very well."

The real problem, he argues, is that schools tend to be large, bureaucratic, and impersonal institutions where kids receive little attention. Small schools, on the other hand, offer students a better sense of community and more attention. "Schools should be restructuring themselves," Mr. Moe says. "They should be small."

Most people agree that there is no simple solution to reducing violence among children. The effort involves schools, parents, and children themselves.

"It's a process. It's a long process," says Lantieri. "But you have to hang in there."

We live within five miles of the place where young Megan Kanka was sexually assaulted and murdered by a neighbor. This terrible crime has stimulated the public cry for what is called "Megan's Law," a federal law designed to ensure that residents are informed should anyone move into their neighborhood or town who has a history of committing sex crimes against children, or who is deemed by the legal system to be a "sexual predator." While civil libertarians and others are testing the legality of this statute, the demand for "Megan's Law" springs from feelings of desperation, fear, and helplessness.

For our family, it struck close to home in many ways. Our own daughter was the same age as Megan, and in the days following the tragic event I faced some troubling questions. What if it had been our child? What can I do as a parent to ensure the safety of our child at all times? For several days I kept a very close, almost obsessive eye on her. Instead of lessening my fears, this reactionary response to the crime inflamed them, leaving me feeling that this dear child was vulnerable if she strayed even momentarily from my sight. This was unhealthy for both of us and had to stop.

As I was praying for direction on how to be loosed from the grip of this constant fear for her safety, a poem entitled "Nice Snake!" that once appeared in *The Christian Science Monitor* (Oct. 23, 1991) came to thought. The poem by Godfrey John told the story of an actual child in South Africa who was sitting on her porch eating a bowl of cereal when a boa constrictor began to wrap its coils around her and her chair. Innocently, the child offered it a spoonful of milk, which it drank. But when the snake dipped its head into the bowl of cereal, the child tapped it on the head with her spoon and said: "Naughty, naughty! Wait your turn!" She continued to feed both herself and the snake by turns. When they came to the bottom of the bowl, the snake unwrapped itself from the child and slipped quietly off the porch.

Protecting Children from Sudden Harm

Michelle Boccanfuso

Contributor
Christian Science Sentinel

I love this story for its illustration of the child's innocent thought—her genuine love and pure affection—which clearly protected her from any aggressive tendencies of the snake. Rather than become a victim of the boa, the child found it to be a responsive breakfast companion. Her calm authority in the situation illustrated her dominion over fear.

Such spiritual poise points to the presence and power of the Christ, the true idea of God, in human consciousness. Christ Jesus spoke of man's ability to overcome evil tendencies when he said, "Behold, I give unto you power to tread on serpents and scorpions, and over all the power of the enemy: and nothing shall by any means hurt you" (Luke 10:19).

I couldn't help but wonder what the mother or nanny or whoever might have thought, having discovered the child and the snake just as they were finishing the cereal. This really got me thinking. How was I watching our daughter? Was I looking only for danger so that I might be able to ward it off? Is that an effective way to watch? Or could it be that the greater need includes not losing sight of the purity, innocence, and love that are innate to everyone as God's child? Did I need to cultivate my understanding of the protective laws of God and the spiritual power that companions with and sustains all of God's innocent children?

It is helpful to know that God is the universal and divine Parent of all. *Science and Health with Key to the Scriptures* by Mary Baker Eddy states, "Love, the divine Principle, is the Father and Mother of the universe, including man" (p. 256). True safety and security for our children rest on the practical understanding that God is the loving and eternal Parent of man. He neither creates nor condones evil, and a correct understanding of Him eliminates evil as an undermining influence in our lives.

The book of Isaiah describes the innocency of God's creation, and the protection and peace that accompany pure, loving, childlike thought: "The sucking child shall play on the hole of the asp, and the weaned child shall put his hand on the cockatrice's den. They shall not hurt nor destroy in all my holy mountain: for the earth shall be full of the knowledge of the Lord, as the waters cover the sea" (11:8, 9). Because God is the Father and Mother of the universe, we are never separated for an instant from our divine Parent. There is no lapse in His child's innocence, spirituality, and dominion over all evil.

It occurred to me that the spiritual demand was to remember that my daughter's innocence was indeed her best defense against evil. I knew that with this kind of watching, keeping her wholly spiritual and undefilable nature in my sights, I could be assured of her perpetual safety and security. This brought me great peace.

Over the next few days, I began watching our daughter in this completely new way, not losing sight of the fact that she was God's innocent child. I saw a need to establish in our home a regular time each day when we would read the Bible and discuss the evidence of God's care and protection as illustrated in the lives of Biblical figures. This special time together served to deepen our mutual understanding of the power of childlike innocence and the ever-present protecting influence of God. The fear of some evil lurking in our neighborhood lost its grip as we both became more aware of man's invulnerability to evil as God's beloved child. The feelings of helplessness fled when I realized I could be proactive in protecting our daughter by nurturing the spiritual innocence that she naturally possessed.

Spiritual innocence is a strength. The innocent thought recognizes the rules of goodness and follows them faithfully. Innocence is conscious intelligence, such as was exhibited by the child who fearlessly tapped the snake on the head with her spoon. The spiritually innocent thought is invulnerable to evil because it understands good is the governing power, the only power.

We can support children's natural, intelligent expression of innocence by helping them form habits of obedience to God, by nurturing their understanding of and love for His law of good, and by showing them how to turn consistently to Him for wisdom in daily decision making.

The understanding that God is the true Parent of our children as well as our neighbors' does not lessen an individual parent's responsibility to provide a safe and secure environment. Parents should take practical steps to keep their children safe, and appropriate laws should be passed and enforced to ensure the highest degree of legal protection for children. But it is also important to be conscious of and take active part in each child's spiritual development. Parents can support their children's blossoming understanding of man's innocence, purity, and love as an actual protective influence coming from God. Then we are providing children with the most effective defense against evil, seen or unseen.

How Does God See This Child?

Yvonne M.
Trankle

Contributor
Christian Science Sentinel

Rather than eating in the teachers' lounge, I often had lunch in my classroom while grading papers. This particular day, however, I ate in the lounge, and the conversation centered on discipline, with many bemoaning the fact that their methods of handling serious discipline problems weren't working. My thought was drifting when suddenly one of the teachers turned to me and asked, "Well, what's the answer?" I was taken aback and thought at first that she wasn't really expecting an answer. But then I realized I indeed had the answer because I had proved it, so I piped up: "I do have the answer. It's unconditional love." I then related a short version of the following experience.

Just before summer vacation one year, I was given my class list for the following school year. As I looked at the names, my heart sank, for among them was the name of a girl I had heard every year since she was in kindergarten. She was known as being very disruptive and rebellious. In fact, no one ever had a kind word to say about her. Previously I had almost left the teaching profession because of a similar student, and I knew I needed to do a lot of growing (spiritually) in order to meet this challenge. My thought now was "Either I can spend my whole summer worrying about this, or I can study the Bible and *Science and Health* and gain the spiritual understanding needed to heal this situation." I chose the latter.

I realized I had a lot of fear to overcome—fear of rejection, fear of loss of control in front of the class, fear of not being able to handle this. (Nine months in school would seem like an eternity if this wasn't healed.) But in looking up references on Love, I found this powerful promise in *Science and Health*: "Love must triumph over hate" (p. 43). And further on it states, "Clad in the panoply of Love, human hatred cannot reach you" (*ibid.*, p. 571). Not only was I being assured of victory, I was being told I couldn't even be touched by hatred—divine Love was my protection. The fact is, the very essence of man's being is divine Love because God, or Love, created man as His reflection. At that point I realized that I needn't have any fear, and that instead of worrying about myself, my role as Love's reflection was to help this student.

I used the concordances to Mary Baker Eddy's writings to look up every reference to child and children. When I read this passage, ". . . the author has often remembered our Master's love for little children, and understood how truly such as they belong to the heavenly kingdom," I had my answer (*ibid.*, p. 130). There were no conditions that children had to meet before they could be loved. Jesus didn't love only children who acted a certain way—he loved all of them unconditionally because he was seeing them only in their true, spiritual state of being, as expressions of purity and innocence. I realized that I needed to raise my human concept of love to a more spiritual, Christly love. In order to do this, I needed to reject all the gossip I had heard about this child and realize this was not her true nature. I found myself asking, "How does God see this child?"

This was a humbling question. I was ashamed I had been taken in by the picture of an angry, out-of-control child. As I continued my study, it became clear that God could see this child only as He sees all His children as they really are—sinless, innocent, loving, lovable, and receptive. I further reasoned that since I was the likeness of God, I had the ability to see this child as God did, to love unconditionally.

I gleaned further insight from part of a description of Gethsemane in *Science and Health,* describing the Christ-love, which never stops loving, even in the face of crucifixion: ". . . the human yielding to the divine; love meeting no response, but still remaining love" (p. 586). I didn't have to worry about how this child responded to me. I simply had to be so filled with God's love that it wouldn't matter how she behaved toward me, because no matter what she said or did, I would still love her. I was beginning to grasp what unconditional love truly is.

During those months of study, I gained a clear picture of this child's true identity. I saw her as a loving and intelligent spiritual idea. I saw that divine Love is the only power and that it would melt away the supposed power of hatred, resistance, or hardness. I had an expectancy of good. By the time I was in my classroom getting it ready for the start of school, I was prepared to welcome her with open arms.

I didn't have long to wait. She appeared outside my window fifteen minutes after my arrival. I smiled, greeted her by name, and said, "I'm looking forward to having you in my class." Her mouth dropped open slightly, she mumbled something, and left. I wasn't sure what that meant, but I was sure I genuinely loved her.

The first day of school went smoothly with hardly a peep from this particular student. At recess, she came and stood by me for a while and then said, "Did you really mean what you said about wanting me in your class?" I assured her I did. She repeated that question several times over the next few days. There were no behavior problems. She was cooperative, helpful, and did well academically. It was so noticeable that other teachers commented about the change. By the time she entered fifth grade, her new teachers, having witnessed her change in behavior, no longer feared disruption, and there was never any mention of her previous bad record.

Yes, I had found the answer. It was Christlike, unconditional love, and the response had been immediate. So well did I learn that lesson, that I never again had a student I was even tempted to dislike. I was able to apply what I had learned to all children. I no longer felt I had to be stern or fight for control. Instead, discipline was established with an ease I had not thought possible. You see, the healing power of Christ-love is irresistible. It is capable of overcoming any obstacle, changing viewpoints and changing lives.

Chapter 9

Being

an Active Safeguarder

Helping Out America's Youths– Family-Style: Volunteer "Summit" Will Press Need for More Adult Mentors

Scott Baldauf

With Assistance
from Alexandra Marks
and Staff Writers
The Christian Science Monitor

WASHINGTON, D.C.—Now, volunteering to help a troubled youngster can be a family affair.

From Philadelphia to Oakland, California, volunteer agencies are encouraging adult mentors to bring youngsters home to experience life in a stable, two-parent family. Unlike the traditional one-on-one mentoring approach, "family mentoring" can enable people to give to their communities while still spending treasured free time with their own children.

Family mentoring signals a new flexibility by volunteer agencies to accommodate busy schedules of today's volunteers. It's one way of addressing the nation's need for more adult mentors—a dominant theme of 1997's star-studded presidential "summit" in Philadelphia.

The summit on volunteerism featured most of America's political luminaries, who put shoulder to spade on opening day to spruce up a park in one of the city's low-income neighborhoods. Their effort was intended, too, to lay the groundwork for today, when presidents past and present will mount the stairs of Independence Hall in a united bid to revitalize the country's sense of civic responsibility.

The steady commitment of an adult's time is one of the most powerful forces in turning kids around, experts say. A recent survey of the nation's five largest Big Brothers/Big Sisters programs found that at-risk teens who had mentors were 46 percent less likely to start using drugs, 27 percent less likely to start using alcohol, 52 percent less likely to skip school, and 33 percent less likely to get into fights. And even though the mentors rarely helped children with their schoolwork, grades improved 3 percent.

"The rise in grades may look pretty small, but it took us by surprise," says Gary Walker of Public/Private Ventures in Philadelphia, which conducted the study. Even so, "it confirmed a suspicion we had, that simply having an adult in their lives can make a difference."

138

Tapping the strong, natural urge to please an adult can be the best way to keep at-risk children on the straight and narrow path, experts say. Summit organizers put the number of at-risk children—who live in poor families, often with a single parent—at 15 million.

"In California, we interviewed 100 kids who made it back after years of getting into trouble with drugs and alcohol," says Andrew Mecca of the California Mentoring Initiative, a public-private partnership in Sacramento. "The thing . . . that made the difference was that someone held aspirations for them."

But as the work week grows longer, many adults feel unable to commit some of their scant free time. Family mentoring breaks down this barrier, says Debra Lambrecht of the Caring About Kids mentoring program in Auburn, California. "It benefits not just the youth and their families, but the mentoring families as well."

Family mentoring is just one of the new methods being used to attract busy volunteers. Another approach is "team mentoring," in which volunteers form a partnership with other adults and take turns looking after a set of kids. One partner may focus on character, another on community service, and another on helping children choose their career paths.

But while volunteer groups are changing their strategies to attract younger adults, the bulk of volunteer work is being carried out by retirees, who have both time and civic spirit.

In Philadelphia, retiree Ethel Taylor gives three or four hours a week, meeting with a sixth-grade girl to help build her confidence in school. The work must be paying off, because Mrs. Taylor's youngster recently won a trophy in a public speaking contest.

Nearby, Harold Watson spends several hours a week with a seventh-grade boy. They go out to eat together, attend soccer games, and drive out to the airport and watch the airplanes take off. Most of all, they talk. "He says he wants to be a pilot," says Mr. Watson, a retired community activist, "and I told him, 'You have to get A's and B's and be serious about your studies. Pilots have a lot of responsibility.'"

Watson says Americans could donate more of their time to the community if they spent less time in front of the television. "What good is time if it isn't used productively?" he asks. "For myself, I just feel better as a person that the attention I'm giving is making a difference."

Launching the presidential summit in Philadelphia, volunteers were up at dawn on April 27, in the Germantown section, shovels, rakes, and paint brushes in hand. They're transforming a neighborhood park from a drab, neglected corner of beaten-down grass to a bright, cheerful center for children to play.

Power tools are humming as volunteers erect bright blue-and-red monkey bars and jungle gyms. The neighborhood kids helped design the park in conjunction with KaBoom, a Washington-based nonprofit agency that builds playgrounds around the country.

Gary Pawlovich, a father of five from Bucks County, Pennsylvania, is holding up a cast-iron support. This is the first time he's volunteered in years, in part because he and his family have moved six times in the past 20 years.

"It's hard to build up relationships in a community when you're moving so much, and community projects have suffered as a result," says Mr. Pawlovich, who works for the corporation that is underwriting the playground construction. Volunteering has given him a sense of satisfaction, he says, but also a greater awareness of the challenges faced by low-income communities like Germantown.

Is active, conspicuous love for children and teenagers a top priority? Are we willing to make a long-term commitment? Children, teenagers, young adults—all young people require advocates. In coming years throughout the United States, over a billion dollars' worth of public service advertising will be spent annually asking "Whose side are you on?" That's more than for any other Advertising Council campaign ever.

Education and opportunities for young people, violence and abuse, health care and maintenance, economic growth and the deficit—these are just some of the issues behind the question "Whose side are you on?" More than just a noble appeal for people to stop abusing children, to stop exploiting them, to cease resenting them, the question impels people to reassess their priorities.

Consent to making the well-being of children, teenagers, and young adults an ongoing priority takes some courage and persistence. The demands of our lives are sometimes so absorbing and things so complicated and difficult that it may seem we can barely hold our own head above water much less help others. Often, though, people have found that helping others offers benefits and dividends that go far beyond the effort and time invested.

The part we all can beneficially play in the well-being of children is so important that it is natural for many people to turn to God for guidance. When confronted with increasingly difficult responsibilities in guiding others, the Bible's Solomon prayed, "Give therefore thy servant an understanding heart to judge thy people, that I may discern between good and bad" (I Kings 3:9). It's easy to relate to those words today and to ask God to help us also, to give us "an understanding heart," so we can know how to help in the way that will do the most good.

One of the best ways to start answering the question "Whose side are you on?" is to consider looking

Whose Side Are You On?

Mark Swinney

Contributing Editor
Christian Science Sentinel

at the young people around us from a spiritual perspective, from the perspective of how God has created all children. What kind of children are we talking about? God's perfect, spiritually created child. This is the side we're on! But how do we see this child of God? Through limited, mortal sight and thought? We have to look with our hearts, from our deepest, loving standpoint, at God's perfection and at God's perfect, spiritual offspring—pure, gentle, strong, and cared for. Then consistently beholding God's child has a healing effect. That's because thought determines the nature of our environment. To love and see God's goodness expressed in all children is a form of prayer; that actually brings the healing, protecting law of God to everything we experience.

There is so much to discover about God's child. As we acknowledge God's goodness and power, God's creation is revealed more and more. God is all-powerful and always present with us, directing our steps toward what will help children in the most practical, healing ways. We can always act on God's direction with confidence as we feel His power and love. Productive, progressive steps become clearer—steps that truly help bring about change for the better.

In fact, the less we depend on ourselves and the more we look humbly to God, the more we'll help not only others but ourselves. The woman who founded this magazine almost one hundred years ago, Mary Baker Eddy, prayed, using the image of a shepherd as a metaphor for God,

> Shepherd, show me how to go
> O'er the hillside steep,
> How to gather, how to sow,—
> How to feed Thy sheep . . . .
> (Poems, p. 14)

To look to the Shepherd, divine Mind, shows us how to feed all children with encouragement, patience, with good morals and ethics, and especially with an understanding of God's great love for everyone. As we express God in the minutiae of our daily lives, we put an example, a model, before the world that can help others discover the ways God's loving law operates in their own lives. Everyone has the power of God, "the kingdom of heaven," within himself or herself.

The prayer just discussed ends like this:

> So, *when day grows dark and cold,*
> *Tear or triumph harms,*
> *Lead Thy lambkins to the fold,*
> *Take them in Thine arms;*
> *Feed the hungry, heal the heart,*
> *Till the morning's beam;*
> *White as wool, ere they depart,*
> *Shepherd, wash them clean.*

With God's help, can't anyone play a part, large or small, in feeding the hungry and healing the heart of young people? Seeing a child as God knows him or her is the most loving way you can do this. Practical, progressive steps naturally follow. The children, teenagers, and young adults of today and for all the future deserve this kind of love. Through God's guidance, we each can discover opportunities to contribute to a young person's growth—and rejoice in it.

Appendix A

Internet Sites
Related to Children's Safety Issues

"Safeguarding the Children" Site Announced by The Christian Science Publishing Society

This site includes links to articles from *The Christian Science Monitor, The Christian Science Journal, Christian Science Sentinel,* and *Christian Science Sentinel— Radio Edition.*

http://www.tfccs.com/GV/ Children/Children.html

NOTE: The Christian Science Publishing Society does not endorse the sites behind the following list of links. We offer them for your additional research. The Internet is constantly changing, so some of these sites may no longer exist.

TV Violence

UCLA TV Violence Monitoring Project
http://www.ucla.edu/current/hotline/violence/i.htm

US Kids Television and Anti-Violence Campaign
http://www.axsamer.org/~uskidstv/

Kill Your TV—Violence Statistics
http://www.localaccess.com/
    hardebeck/killtv2.htm#Violence

Frontline/Does TV Kill? Teacher's Guide
http://www2.pbs.org/wgbh/pages/
    frontline/fltvkillguide.html

Center for Media Literacy
http://websites.earthlink.net/~cml/cml.html

Teaching Media Literacy
http://interact.uoregon.edu/MediaLit/
    FA/MLCurriculum/Menu

Directory: Media Literacy Organizations
http://interact.uoregon.edu/MediaLit/FA/MLDirectory

Teen Peer Pressure/Gangs

Bureau of Justice Statistics Homepage
http://www.ojp.usdoj.gov/bjs/

Crime Statistics Site
http://www.crime.org/

Rate Your Risk
http://www.Nashville.Net/~police/risk/

Federal Gang Violence Act
http://www.senate.gov/member/ca/feinstein/
    general/gangs.html

Family Problems/Crises

Dysfunctional Families—Related Articles
http://www.missouri.edu:80/~councwww/self_help/topic_8/index.html

The Family Violence Prevention Fund
http://www.igc.apc.org/fund/

Department of Health and Human Services, Administration
for Children and Families
http://www.acf.dhhs.gov/

Higher Education Center Against Violence and Abuse
http://www.umn.edu/mincava/

Crisis Nursery Care
http://www.chtop.com/archfs1.htm

Group Plans for Crisis Nursery
http://www.bslnet.com/accounts/frepress/www/march/d.html

Kare for Kids Crisis Nursery for Homeless Children
http://www.rdgroup.com/nashville/Kare.htm

Sexual Exploitation of Children

Congress Against Sexual Exploitation of Children Home Page
http://www.childhub.ch/webpub/csechome/

Convention on the Rights of the Child
http://www.unicef.org/crc/

SF Bay Guardian: Protecting Children
http://www.sfbayguardian.com/Politics/96_06/060596oped.html

Safety from Guns and Peer Violence on Streets,
at School, at Home

Not One More
http://www.frisk.com/not/

Increasing Adolescent Violence
http://sunsite.unc.edu/horizon/pastissues/preview/social1.html

Report on Youth and Violence
http://www1.cc.emory.edu/EMORY_REPORT/erarchive/
    1995/October/ERoct.30/10.30.952nd.rep.youth.html

"No Weapons on Campus,"
a page on the Los Angeles Unified School District
http://www.lausd.k12.ca.us/police/weapons/

Police Department Web Site
http://www.lausd.k12.ca.us/police/

Los Angeles Times Web Site
http://www.latimes.com/

Shootings Renew Concern About Violence at Schools
http://mbhs.bergtraum.k12.ny.us/cybereng/nyt/sch-vio.htm

Home, School, and Neighborhood Conflict Resolution

Conflict Resolution Suggestions for Parents
http://www.onr.com/tpta/conflict.html

The Conflict Resolution Process
http://www.commnet.edu/QVCTC/classes/conflict/weeks.html

Resolving Conflict Creatively Program
http://www.benjerry.com/esr/index.html

Soulforce
http://www.fabian-baber.com/soulforce/

Resolving Conflict Peacefully
http://www.nwrel.org/newsletters/prev/wc_news/dec95/conflict.html

It's All Problem Solving
http://www.nea.org/resource/tips.html

Teen Conflict Homepage
http://www.commnet.edu/QVCTC/classes/conflict/teenhome.html

Internet Dangers

Atlanta Man Sentenced in International Computer
Child Pornography Case
http://www.law.emory.edu/USAO/news/everett.html

Pornography Police Versus the Internet
http://www.ix.de/ct/Artikel/96/02/Zensur_eng.htm

Campaigning Against Juvenile Prostitution
http://www.uia.org/uiademo/str/u1527.htm

National Center for Missing and Exploited Children
http://www.missingkids.org/

Internet "Filtering" Issues and Software Providers*

SurfWatch Software's SurfWatch
800-458-6600
http://www.surfwatch.com

Cyber Patrol from Microsystems Software
800-489-2001
http://www.microsys.com

NewView Inc.'s Specs for Kids
http://www.newview.com

Solid Oak Software's CYBERSitter
805-967-9853
http://www.solidoak.com

InterGo's KinderGuard
972-424-7882
http://www.intergo.com

Trove Investment Corp.'s Net Nanny
800-340-7177
http://www.netnanny.com

---

* These sites may also be found in the "Safe Surfing" article in Chapter 5.

Turner Investigation, Research, and Communication and J.D. Koftinoff
Software Ltd.'s Internet Filter (Canada, British Columbia)
604-708-2397
http://www.turnercom.com

Net Shepherd Inc.'s daxHOUND (Canada, Alberta)
403-218-8900
http://www.netshepherd.net

Internet Sites about the Web and Children*

SafeSurf
http://www.safesurf.com

Recreational Software Advisory Council
http://www.rsac.org

Project OPEN
http://www.isa.net/project-open/empower.html

Larry Magid's Kids Page
http://www.larrysworld.com/kids.html

SAFE-T-CHILD On-line
http://www.yellodyno.com

The Internet Advocate
http://www.monroe.lib.in.us/~lchampel/netadv.html

---

* These sites may also be found in the "Safe Surfing" article in Chapter 5.

Appendix B

Sources
of Articles

1. Working to Keep Children Safe

Working with Young People to Make Their Lives Safer
The Christian Science Monitor, September 23, 1996

Culprits Are Alcohol, Drugs, Parental Actions, Teens Say
The Christian Science Monitor, September 23, 1996

Teens Speak Out
The Christian Science Monitor, September 23, 1996

Children Are Not Victims
The Christian Science Monitor, September 4, 1996

Cherishing the World's Children
Christian Science Sentinel, September 30, 1996

2. Stopping Family Violence

Efforts to End Abuse Open Doors for Troubled Families
The Christian Science Monitor, December 30, 1996

Connecting the Dots: Men Find Antidote for Anger
The Christian Science Monitor, December 30, 1996

Crisis Nurseries Help Parents in Tough Times
The Christian Science Monitor, December 30, 1996

Freedom from Past Abuse: Through Regression? Or Progression?
The Christian Science Journal, September, 1996

3. Countering the Danger of Guns

What Makes Children Choose to Use Guns?
The Christian Science Monitor, October 7, 1996

One Family's Trials Spur a Commitment to Community Safety
The Christian Science Monitor, October 7, 1996

Schools Get Results with Gun-Free Zones
The Christian Science Monitor, October 7, 1996

School Shootings—and Individual Prayer
Christian Science Sentinel, September 23, 1996

4. Dealing with the Media and Its Messages

Battles Over Media Violence Move to a New Frontier: The Internet
The Christian Science Monitor, November 18, 1996

More Parents Turn to an Old-Fashioned V-Chip: Themselves
The Christian Science Monitor, November 18, 1996

Beyond Blame: Media Literacy at Work
The Christian Science Monitor, November 18, 1996

Superseding the Hollywood "Ministry of Culture"
The Christian Science Monitor, November 18, 1996

A New Approach to Education—for the Safety of Children
The Christian Science Journal, September, 1996

5. Protecting Children from Internet Dangers

"Off-Line" Hazards Lie in Web's Links, Lures
The Christian Science Monitor, August 29, 1996

Safe Surfing: Ways to Guide a Child's Web Use
The Christian Science Monitor, August 29, 1996

Some Rules of the Road for the Information Superhighway
The Christian Science Monitor, August 29, 1996

Praying to Stop Child Abuse
The Christian Science Monitor, September 18, 1996

6. Battling the Child Sex Trade

Sex Trade Lures Kids from Burbs
The Christian Science Monitor, August 30, 1996

Getting Adults to Think in New Ways
The Christian Science Monitor, September 16, 1996

You Didn't Deserve to Be Hurt
Christian Science Sentinel, September 2, 1996

Innocence in the City
Christian Science Sentinel, September 23, 1996

7. Resisting Drugs, Alcohol, and Peer Pressure

Santa Barbara Aims to Knock Out Drug Abuse by "Fighting Back"
The Christian Science Monitor, December 2, 1996

It Takes a Community to Fight Drug Abuse
The Christian Science Monitor, December 2, 1996

A Tough Sell: Breaking Away from Gangs
The Christian Science Monitor, December 16, 1996

Being There for Your Children
The Christian Science Journal, September, 1996

School in Safety
Christian Science Sentinel, September 9, 1996

8. Defusing Neighborhood Conflict

Neighborhood Defense: Watchful Eyes, Caring Hearts
The Christian Science Monitor, October 21, 1996

Schools Try Conflict Resolution to Help Students Stay Focused on Facts, Not Fights
The Christian Science Monitor, October 21, 1996

Protecting Children from Sudden Harm
Christian Science Sentinel, September 23, 1996

How Does God See This Child?
Christian Science Sentinel, September 9, 1996

9. Being an Active Safeguarder

Helping Out America's Youth — Family-Style
The Christian Science Monitor, April 28, 1997

Whose Side Are You On?
Christian Science Sentinel, December 30, 1996

Appendix

C

Publications
Information

The Christian Science Monitor

An international daily newspaper founded in 1908 by Mary Baker Eddy. The *Monitor* has won six Pulitzer Prizes and innumerable other awards from such organizations as Sigma Delta Chi, the Overseas Press Club, the American Society of Newspaper Editors, the National Press Photographer's Association, and the National Association of Black Journalists. An article published by the Gannett Foundation Media Center at Columbia University cited the *Monitor* as one of the top six newspapers in the United States and top twenty in the world, for its "solid quality and intellectual perspective." The *Monitor* is published in print, and on the Internet at http://www.csmonitor.com/.

The Christian Science Journal

A monthly publication of the First Church of Christ, Scientist. It contains reports of healing, inspirational articles, editorials, features, poems, and important church news. Each issue also includes a worldwide directory of Christian Science churches and their services, Christian Science organizations at colleges and universities, practitioners, teachers, nurses, and Committees on Publication.

Christian Science Sentinel

A weekly magazine focusing on contemporary issues and spiritual solutions, with features, poems, editorials, and reports of healing. The magazine illustrates the practical relevance of an understanding of God in finding answers to individual and societal problems. It also includes Christian Science lecture schedules. A radio edition of the *Sentinel* is broadcast weekly on shortwave and by various radio stations around the United States and overseas.

The Christian Science Publishing Society

The Publishing Society is a trust established by Mary Baker Eddy for the publication of the *Christian Science Quarterly*, *The Christian Science Journal*, the *Christian Science Sentinel*, the *Herald of Christian Science*, and other periodicals, such as *The Christian Science Monitor*, and general publications including approximately 300 titles of books, pamphlets, leaflets, cassettes, videos, and other items.

The First Church of Christ, Scientist

Also referred to as The Mother Church, has administrative offices in Boston, Massachusetts, activities worldwide, and a web site at http://www.tfccs.com. Approximately 2,200 branch churches of The Mother Church are located throughout the world.

Christian Science Reading Room

A bookstore, usually including a place to read or study, where the writings of Mary Baker Eddy, the Bible and Bible reference books, and other literature published or sold by The Christian Science Publishing Society may be purchased. Librarians, who are local Christian Scientists in charge of Reading Rooms, are available to answer questions.

- To subscribe to *The Christian Science Monitor,*
  call toll-free 1-800-456-2220.
- To subscribe to *The Christian Science Journal* or *Christian Science Sentinel,* call toll-free 1-800-456-4851.

Index

Trankle, Yvonne M., 134–136
Trotta, Laurie, 53
TRUCE (Teachers for Resisting Unhealthy
        Children's Entertainment), 52–53
Turecki, Stanley, 24
Turn-in (buy-back) programs
        for guns, 33, 35
Turvey, John, 80
Tyler, Toby, 66–67

U

United Methodist Church, 20, 127
United Nations Committee for UNICEF, 90
United Nations Convention on the Rights of
        the Child, 84

V

V-chip, 46, 48, 52
Video games, 46
Vining, Barbara M., 59–62
Violence
        causes of, 2–3
        children's desensitization to, 3–4
        children's fears concerning, 3, 6
        children's learning, 6, 9
        families and. See Domestic violence
        gun-free zones in schools and, 38–40
        impact on children of, 47
        Internet and portrayal of, 46, 49–50
        Internet sites on, 147–148
        need of children to feel safe and threat
                of, 2
        parents and, 6
        prevalence of, 3
        school programs on, 34, 36
        in schools, 3, 41
        statistics concerning children and, 2

Volunteers, 138–140
        after-school programs and, 126–127
        family mentoring and, 138–139
        school programs and, 124–125
        team mentoring and, 139
        Walker, Channing, 115–118

W

Walker, Gary, 138
Walsh, David, 51–52, 53
Walt Disney Home Video, 88
WARN (Weapons Are Removed Now), 39–40
Watson, Harold, 139
Weapons. See Guns
Weapons Are Removed Now (WARN), 39–40
Westley, Laurie, 38
Westman, Jack C., 115
WHISPER (Women Harmed in Systems of
        Prostitution Engaged in Revolt), 89, 93
White, Daphne, 53
White, Ted, 24
Women
        anger-management programs for men and,
                22–23
        violence against. See Domestic violence
Women Harmed in Systems of Prostitution
        Engaged in Revolt (WHISPER), 89, 93
Woodruff, Sarah, 51
World Council of Churches, 20
World Wide Web, 64–65. See also Internet

Y

Youth. See Children; Teens
Youth Crime Watch of America, 5
Youth Nonviolence Training Program (YNTP),
        129
Youth to Youth, 4